Ethical Dilemmas in Education

Standing Up for Honesty and Integrity

Beverley H. Johns,
Mary Z. McGrath, and
Sarup R. Mathur

Rowman & Littlefield Education
Lanham • New York • Toronto • Plymouth, UK
2008

Published in the United States of America
by Rowman & Littlefield Education
A division of Rowman & Littlefield Publishers, Inc.
A wholly owned subsidiary of The Rowman & Littlefield Publishing Group, Inc.
4501 Forbes Boulevard, Suite 200, Lanham, Maryland 20706
www.rowmaneducation.com

Estover Road, Plymouth PL6 7PY, United Kingdom

British Library Cataloguing in Publication Information Available

Library of Congress Cataloging-in-Publication Data
Johns, Beverley H. (Beverley Holden)
    Ethical dilemmas in education : standing up for honesty and integrity /
Beverley H. Johns, Mary Z. McGrath, and Sarup R. Mathur.
        p. cm.
    Includes bibliographical references.
    ISBN-13: 978-1-57886-782-0 (cloth : alk. paper)
    ISBN-10: 1-57886-782-7 (cloth : alk. paper)
    ISBN-13: 978-1-57886-783-7 (pbk. : alk. paper)
    ISBN-10: 1-57886-783-5 (pbk. : alk. paper)
    1. Teachers—Professional ethics. 2. Education—Moral and ethical aspects. 3.
Teaching—Moral and ethical aspects. I. McGrath, Mary Z., 1947– II. Mathur,
Sarup R. III. Title.
    LB1779.J64 2008
    174'.937—dc22   2007046335

To all educators who strive to raise
the integrity of the broader school culture
through their individual ethical actions

Contents

CHAPTER 1

Ethical Dilemmas in Education

Margaret is a longtime educator of 25 years at Pleasant Valley Middle School. She adheres to the values of integrity and honesty. Sometimes her colleagues think she is too much of a "goody two-shoes" and joke with her to just lighten up. For years, the school's tradition has been to have a holiday party before the winter break at the home of the principal. There is a new principal this year—significantly younger than the long-term principal who retired at the end of the last year.

Margaret has not felt comfortable with this new principal but is unsure why. Her gut-level feeling is that his moral values are not the same as hers. The principal seems to brag a lot about the parties he has at his house but doesn't come out and say why his parties are so much fun. In keeping with tradition, she goes to the holiday party. When she arrives, she immediately notices that the liquor is abundant, and some of the individuals are already getting drunk.

The principal then announces that it is time for special gifts that he has gotten the staff. The gifts are wrapped, and when each teacher opens his or hers, the gifts are of a sexual nature—sexual toys, skimpy underwear. When Margaret opens her gift, she finds a book entitled How to Lighten Up and Have Some Porn Fun. *Margaret is very offended but is torn by what she should do—should she walk out, should she report what has happened to the school superintendent? The other staff members are laughing about all the gifts. She is feeling bothered and goes up to the principal and quietly says she is offended by the gift and is going to leave the party. The principal announces very loudly that Margaret is so prim and proper, and she just doesn't know how to have fun. Everybody laughs; Margaret leaves.*

Over the holiday break, Margaret worries about what she should do. She knows if she reports the situation to the superintendent, she will face the wrath of the principal the rest of the year. Yet, she knows his behavior was way out of line.

Margaret is indeed in an ethical dilemma—she knows that what happened is wrong, but she sees that the other staff members are condoning the behavior. She begins to worry about whether she should just go along with the crowd or stand up for what she believes—that educators should be held to the highest standards of behavior. After all, educators are setting the example for our future leaders—the children we serve. She has a moral responsibility to adhere to ethical standards.

Questions of ethics abound in our society and are plentiful in the press. Ethical violations are happening in big business, in politics, and in virtually every segment of our society, so why wouldn't we expect them to be reflected in education? Yet it is most bothersome when such ethical dilemmas are seen in education. After all, educators are public servants hired by school systems that are entrusted with the protection and welfare and education of our most precious commodity—our children. If anything, educators should be held to the highest ethical standards because of their most important role.

Yet, educators are human beings and unfortunately can succumb to the dangers of society's pressures to do whatever it takes to get ahead or to engage in behaviors that are unethical.

Every day these authors are surprised at the violations of ethics that are seen in the educational world—conflicts of interest, engaging in inappropriate behavior to get ahead, using school equipment inappropriately. Pressures today on educators are tremendous, and when individuals are under such stress, they may begin to justify inappropriate actions to compensate for those pressures.

Pressures to meet differing expectations are difficult for teachers—they are torn between what the child needs, what the administrator wants, what the parents want, and what fellow colleagues think should be done. Educators must make difficult choices and must have the ability to utilize good judgment to make appropriate ethical decisions.

We believe that the time has come when we must focus on the importance of ethical behavior for educators. As authors we are bothered by the behaviors we observe in some educators. We have seen educators who have forgotten their purpose in being a teacher; they may have forgotten about the needs of the students or are so wrapped up in their own needs that they don't focus on the child. Some educators will do what it takes to get ahead within the school system even when it means jeopardizing services to the child. Some may ignore the unethical practices or even the illegal practices of their colleagues.

By condoning colleagues' inappropriate behaviors, these individuals are cultivating a culture that allows inappropriate practice. We cannot condone those behaviors and must do our part to curb the tide of the desensitization of ethical and moral behavior. All educators must set the highest standards of values, and those values must be seen in their behavior.

In a recent Broward County, Florida, newspaper article (Renaud, 2006), it was reported that the Broward County Public Schools' Special Investigative Unit found that 50 employees out of the district's 40,000 workers were found to be at fault in incidents that concluded in 2006. Unfortunately these employees ranged from a building principal who engaged in several inappropriate relationships with staff, to a teacher who said she gave some students with disabilities answers to questions on the high-stakes testing, to a teacher who encouraged two students to attack a third in her classroom, to a food service manager who was charged with robbing a bank at gunpoint.

These incidents are occurring at an increasing and alarming rate, yet little is written about ethics in education, and as society faces more questions and problems with ethics, this topic must be addressed in pre-service and in the ongoing training of educators.

It must also be addressed by all of us by doing our part to create and sustain an ethical culture in our schools. This book deals with the issues and how-tos of creating such a culture.

Jennings (2006), an expert in ethics in the business world, has written that most companies have ethics codes and ethics training, but those programs "fall short of taking the steps necessary to create a culture in which employees come forward with concerns and feel comfortable making ethical choices and in which ethics is paramount in decision making" (p. 10).

Jennings' most recent book takes ethics to the next step by making it a critical part of the culture of the organization.

WHAT IS HAPPENING IN TODAY'S SOCIETY?

Why are there more violations of ethical behavior in government, in business, and in education? What has happened in this society? Are we facing an epidemic where ethics is going by the wayside? What are some of the factors that have brought us to where we are today?

Desensitization

Why are we seeing an increase in incidents of unethical behavior occurring in government, business, and education? An analogy can be drawn between the desensitization to violence and to ethics. These authors have spent their careers working with students with challenging behaviors in the public schools. There has been a rise in the severity of incidents of violence in the schools. Why is that? Our society has become desensitized to violence. We see violence continually in the press, on TV and DVDs, and at the theater. We have accepted it as a way of life. We even encourage people to use their fists or weapons to solve problems.

Children from a young age are seeing violence on the TV screen or in computer games. There is so much of it depicted that we have all gotten used to it, and unfortunately it has become a way of life for people who are impressionable.

Likewise, we are becoming desensitized to a lack of ethics. We pick up the newspaper and read about an incident where a government official has engaged in unethical behavior by using his position to lure young pages or staff members. We pick up the newspaper and find a government official who has been convicted of using his authority to provide driver's licenses for unqualified people in exchange for political favors. We pick up the newspaper and learn about a business executive who is charged with embezzling large sums of money from a company. And now, we pick up the newspaper and learn of a teacher who had sex with one of her students. We hear in the news about the building principal who copied the state test questions and disseminated them to the students prior to the test. We begin to see this behavior as a way of life. We become desensitized to it.

The old saying "Nothing surprises me anymore" fits. We are seeing just about everything, and a blur occurs between what our standard of behavior should be versus what is happening in the world around us. Low-level inappropriate behaviors turn into high-level inappropriate behaviors.

Arnold Goldstein, an authority in the area of aggression, wrote a seminal book in 1999 titled *Low-Level Aggression: First Steps on the Ladder to Violence*. His point was that individuals who engage in aggressive behavior start out by engaging in low-level aggression; that aggression is condoned and tolerated. Therefore the individual sees that he can engage in the behavior and not receive any consequences. The individual learns that the behavior is okay and therefore steps it up a notch—because he got away with the behavior, he will take another step on the ladder and engage in a more serious behavior. He gets away with that behavior and proceeds up the ladder until the behavior is so significant that it can no longer be ignored.

These authors see the analogy of unethical behavior and aggression. The individual starts out by engaging in what one would call small unethical behaviors or, as we will discuss later in this book, borderline unethical behavior. The person learns that the behavior may not have any negative consequences, so continues on the path to more blatant unethical behavior.

In the business world, Jennings (2006) has written about the seven signs of ethical collapse. In our way of thinking, these are Goldstein's low-level behaviors that lead to high-level ethical collapse.

One of these seven signs is the belief that goodness in some areas atones for evil in others. Nonprofit organizations are vulnerable because educators may feel noble in their work and therefore may justify unethical behavior. The teacher may say, "I am the teacher; I have the right to do what I want because I am in charge of my classroom." We must be very careful in the classroom that we do not misuse our power and control over our students to engage in unethical behavior. Our positions as educators never give us the right to mistreat children, either physically or emotionally.

Justifying or Rationalizing What You Do

We frequently hear, "Well, everyone else is doing it." As in the case of Margaret, we begin to question our own judgment about what we are doing, when the bottom line is that we know what is the right versus wrong thing to do. We feel as if we have to defend ourselves when we are engaging in ethical behavior.

We must be very careful that we do not go down the dangerous path of doing something because the crowd is doing it. As Jennings (2006) states, we need more individuals with moral courage. Individuals must have the ability to stand up for what they believe is the right thing to do rather than taking the path of least resistance. It is easy to get wrapped up in the culture of the group and to become a follower rather than an independent voice for what is right. This can become a real danger in the school where everyone pretends to work as a "team." If we don't go along with the team, even when the team is engaging in unethical behavior, we are accused of not being a "team player."

Lack of Responsibility—Blaming Others

How many times have we heard someone mutter, "It wasn't my fault"? It is easy for us to place responsibility for our own behavior on someone else. It would have been easy for Margaret to buy into the laughter over the inappropriate gifts—blaming the principal and everyone else for her behavior.

We, as educators, make the choices of whether to engage in ethical behavior or not. We are in control of our own behavior. We cannot control others' actions, but we have a responsibility to make appropriate choices ourselves. We are the ones who are responsible for gathering all the facts, remembering that our purpose is to do what is right to meet the needs of the child and to make a decision based on the facts and the needs of the child.

Apathy—Turning the Other Way

In a survey conducted in 1999, the Society for Human Resource Management found that of employees who saw something illegal or unethical at work, only 66 percent would say something about it (Jennings, 2006). When we ignore behavior that is illegal or unethical, we are condoning that behavior and are hammering another nail into the coffin of the demise of an ethical environment.

Educators may become so wrapped up in survival in a toxic school culture that they become burned out and apathetic about what is surrounding them. Educators may fear retaliation if they speak up and report unethical behavior. If the teacher is new to the school system, she may fear that she will not receive tenure. If the teacher is not new to the system, he may fear that he will be reassigned to a less desirable classroom.

WHAT IS ETHICS?

Dobrin (2002) discussed that ethics isn't preference or inclination. It is about an ethical approach to living. He argues that many voices compete for our attention about what is ethical. We must use our best judgment in determining the ethical course of action. After gathering all of the information needed, we apply our judgment and make the decision about what is ethical.

Every day we make choices in schools—sometimes we have to make very hard choices dealing with the needs of students or ourselves or our colleagues. Good choices result from good judgment.

Across the country, state legislatures have established or are establishing ethics measures designed to ensure honesty and accountability in government (*State Officials and Employees Ethics Act*, 2003). Ethics commissions receive complaints and investigate those complaints. Those acts deal with a variety of topics including conflicts of interests, prohibited activities, use of public property, and protections for whistle-blowers.

Those measures apply to education, but how many educators are actually trained in ethical procedures, and how many schools have policies and procedures on ethical behaviors? How many school systems train their staff on ethics for educators? If such training does occur, is it expected of all individuals, and does a sense of ethics permeate the entire school environment?

Merriam-Webster's Dictionary and Thesaurus (2005) defines ethics as "the code of good conduct for an individual or group." Ethics is defined as conforming to a high standard of morality or virtue and following the accepted rules of moral conduct. *Oxford American Dictionary* (1980) defines ethics as moral philosophy, moral principles. Lastly, *Webster's New*

World Dictionary (2003) defines ethics as the study of standards of conduct and moral judgment.

Ethics is a system of morals of a particular person. *Ethics* is often used synonymously with *morals*, which Webster's defines as being capable of distinguishing between right and wrong.

Ethical behavior is not using our power and control in the classroom to intimidate or harm students. Ethical behavior is not using our position to gain more personal power. Ethical behavior is not engaging in behaviors that are a conflict of interest. Ethical behavior is not lying about our background in order to gain a position. Ethical behavior is not using school property for personal interest.

Ethical behavior is treating students with respect and dignity. Ethical behavior is representing who we are accurately. Ethical behavior is recognizing when we may have a conflict of interest and disclosing that information. Ethical behavior is using school property for school use. Ethical behavior is collecting sufficient information to make an informed decision on behalf of each student.

Ethics is the ability to know the difference between right and wrong and to act in a way that reflects behavior that is considered right. Multiple decisions are made every minute of the day in the schools as we work with children and their families and our peers in the school. A sense of right and wrong must be ingrained in us, and we cannot afford to even contemplate doing something that we know is wrong or of which we are unsure. If we are unsure about a decision that we are about to make, we must reflect long and hard before we act.

Ethics goes beyond doing just what is legal. An educator may follow the letter of the law but not be acting within an ethical manner. As an example, a teacher may be able to show that she is spending so many minutes per day teaching a particular subject—the schedule reflects that, but upon further investigation, the students are doing independent seat work for the majority of that time and are not being provided instructional time.

Remembering the educational needs of the child and his or her family should be first and foremost in our minds and actions. Doing the right thing for that child should drive our standard of ethics.

SO WHAT MUST EDUCATORS DO TO BE ETHICAL?: DOING OUR PART TO ESTABLISH A CULTURE OF ETHICS

Ethics goes beyond reading the code of ethics. It goes beyond attendance at an in-service. It goes beyond just following the law.

It is a way of life—it is an example we must all set in doing what is right at all times on behalf of the children whose lives we are impacting and molding. It is doing our part to create a culture that tolerates no less than the highest standards of conduct and morality. Every minute of the day, we must remember that we are a role model for the children we teach.

We must follow the ethical code of conduct within our school. Rules without enforcement allow the ethical culture to begin its slippage, which can lead to collapse. Thus there are more violations and dismissal of rules, and those violations lead to collapse.

Hopefully your school has a code of ethics that is to be followed—each educator has the responsibility of following those rules and at the same time, when seeing someone who is not following the code of ethics, reporting violations to the appropriate individuals. We must do our part in preventing ethical lapses and never allow ourselves to lapse into unethical behavior.

Our job is to gather the facts to be able to make a sound decision on what is ethical. Using our professional judgment, we can collect the facts about a situation and weigh all sides of the issue. We know the difference between right and wrong, and we must continually remember those differences when we act.

Too often these authors see educators just take the word of another individual without gathering the facts—we cannot rely on the judgment of others. We have the responsibility to make an informed decision ourselves. Educators must vow that we will act as a role model for the children we serve and for our colleagues.

We often read about creating a positive school culture—that positive school culture is exemplified by an environment that expects and promotes the highest standards of conduct on the part of all staff employed within that school.

Reeves (2007) recently wrote about creating lasting cultural changes in schools and defined four essential leadership elements. For all educators, we must accept a leadership role in establishing the highest ethical standards. In looking at the four leadership elements, three of them can be applied to our role in promoting those ethical standards.

The first step is defining what we will not change—identifying values that must be preserved. Clearly the highest standards of ethics must be preserved. Because others are engaging in behaviors that may be questionable never means that we should do so also.

Unfortunately, we may have heard school personnel say, "Well, everyone else is doing it." Just because they are does not mean we should do so if it jeopardizes our moral integrity.

Recognizing the importance of actions is the second step. Voicing that we abide by the code of ethics or talking a good line at an in-service does not mean that we do it. Our everyday actions in recognizing the difference between right and wrong and doing what is right are what really count.

The third step outlined by Reeves is to use the right change tools for your school or district—the wrong tools are those of power that include threats and coercion and management tools that include only training procedures and measurement systems. Leadership tools include role modeling and vision. Educators serve as role models for students and peers and are teaching children the lifelong habit of ethical behavior.

SUMMARY

Educators should have a vision that they will emulate the virtues of ethics and do so every day of their lives.

The remainder of this book focuses on the ethical dilemmas that educators face every day in their work and provides guidance in handling those tough decisions and doing our part in establishing a culture of ethics.

REFERENCES

Dobrin, A. 2002. *Ethics for everyone: How to increase your moral intelligence.* New York: Wiley.

Goldstein, A. 1999. *Low-level aggression: First steps on the ladder to violence*. Champaign, IL: Research Press.

Jennings, M. 2006. *The seven signs of ethical collapse*. New York: St. Martin's Press.

Merriam-Webster's dictionary and thesaurus. 2005. Springfield, MA: Merriam-Webster.

Oxford American dictionary. 1980. New York: Oxford University Press.

Reeves, D. 2007. How do you change school culture? *Educational Leadership* 64(4): 92, 94.

Renaud, J. P. 2006. Investigators find 50 school workers at fault: Some resign over cases, one jailed in bank robbery. *South Florida Sun-Sentinel*, December 29, 2006.

State Officials and Employees Ethics Act. 5 ILCS 430.

Webster's new world dictionary. 2003. New York: Pocket Books.

CHAPTER 2

Professionalism

Megan Post had thoroughly enjoyed her job as an art teacher in an up-scale suburban elementary school. Then, due to financial cuts, her position was suddenly eliminated. As a result, since Megan held a special education license as well, her district transferred her to the "other side of town" to a very different assignment. Although she did not like the job or the school, Megan decided to keep her employment since her paycheck was the means for her and her husband to travel to a warm climate during winter break.

Late one Friday afternoon, at the end of a challenging week, Megan went to her favorite salon for a haircut by Patrice, an outstanding and top-of-the-line stylist. Sitting in a chair facing the mirror, Megan was aware of Patrice's presence only, as dividers separated them from stylists and clients on either side. As Patrice began to trim Megan's hair, this tired teacher began to relax and talk about her week.

She told Patrice how she missed her former job. She described how she loved the other neighborhood and the professional parents with whom she was able to associate. Following a description of the parents, she talked about how smart and creative the students had been at the other school.

As Patrice restyled Megan's hair, she then contrasted the current school with the former one. Now she had to contend with parents who were, in her opinion "never available" and had no clue about fashion and with students who had serious limitations, likely to never make much out of their lives. On and on she went. The name of her school, the names of students, both first and last, not only entered the ears of her stylist but also, unbeknownst to Megan, floated over and around the dividers and reached the ears of unknown clientele nearby.

Who were the unknown clientele? Did Patrice know any of the families mentioned? Was Megan projecting a positive image of local teachers? Where was her respect for the privacy and dignity of all students?

After Patrice completed the cut and Megan took her last glimpse in the mirror, she stood and proceeded to the counter to pay. She did not notice the disgruntled look on the face of the stylist working behind the left divider. That hardworking stylist, Dana, a single mom, not only worked at the salon but also had begun evening fashion design classes, aiming to increase her income. Her two sons attended Megan's former school. Like their mother, they were talented and creative boys who deeply regretted the loss of the art class and the teacher.

Completely clueless, Megan got into her car, put her cell phone earpiece in place, and drove off. Would her travel agent recommend the Caribbean or Mexican Riviera? What a great escape either would be! At least this job enabled her to get away for some sun.

Dana Matson and her sons lived in one of the few new subsidized apartments on the upscale side of town. This single mom struggled to make the best life for her boys that she could. Had the city not recently allowed their building to be located where it was, her boys would be at the school where Megan now worked. Would they be viewed as the families described by the voice coming over the divider?

Dana left work that day not only feeling angry and sad but also with less trust in the teachers of her district. Many questions went through her mind. Had teachers always been this unethical? How did individuals like Mrs. Post make it through the hiring process? Unfortunately, this woman was not who she projected herself to be. Was she giving her heart to students and families at her current school? How did she get along with her peers?

If Mrs. Post spoke this openly in public, how did she speak about her students and their families in the staff lounge? Dana Matson left with many questions late that afternoon as she drove home to prepare supper for her sons. They meant the world to her, and she was determined that they receive a quality education from people of integrity. Maybe, someday she would run for the school board, but in the meantime . . . certainly Megan Post was not representative of the caliber of teacher in their district. Had ethics always been an issue in education?

THE WORLD CHANGES, BUT DO EDUCATIONAL ETHICS?

Consider the world situation at the start of your career. Much continues to happen in our complex and changing world. This impacts education and educators. The government aims to point education in a direction that from its perspective will be the most advantageous to students.

A variety of persons with varied levels of ethics enter the mix and go into the education profession. As policies and personalities interact and time passes, is education reaching a higher level of ethics so students will receive an optimal education? Perhaps each of us would view this differently based on when we have worked, in what location, and what role we maintain in educational work.

Consider the climate of education before the Individuals with Disabilities Education Act (IDEA). In this era, students with disabilities did not have the protections of the law that give them the key to their education. Consequently, many individuals with a range of talents and disabilities might not have been able to reach their optimal potential.

Would schools today be allowed to dismiss someone so readily? Now in place, IDEA and Section 504 provide for those who face challenges in their education. Has this legislation brought ethics to a new level in terms of providing education for those who need unique adaptations? What has happened for all students over the past decades? Following are perspectives of two educators who have seen the educational pendulum swing over time.

Professor Emeritus Frank Wood, PhD, of the University of Minnesota Department of Educational Psychology and Special Education, states:

Over the past 200 years, we have gradually expanded our definition of the meaning of equality in civil rights. Voting rights have been extended to previously excluded groups although age limits still remain. But, of special importance to educators has been the extension of the principle of equal rights to the enjoyment of public property (e.g., buses, parks, and buildings) and public benefits (e.g., education and health care).

This extension has occurred only recently and is still continuing. Why did it take so long? Probably because established custom tends to trump change based on ethical principle. Only as custom begins to loosen up are changes based on ethics implemented in law.

Consider the right of individuals with physical, mental, or emotional impairments to a "free appropriate public education." Before changes in state and national laws, parents in some school districts kept children with severe impairments at home because the common community perception was that such children were "uneducable." Brave parents who brought their children to school were turned away by teachers and administrators who asserted that it is "common knowledge" that such children "do not benefit from education."

Even after a coalition of parents, progressive educators, and legislators secured passage of the Education for All Handicapped Children Act (now IDEA) in the mid-1970s, some school districts allowed administrators to exclude or limit the access to education of individual students. For example, some districts denied equal education opportunities to students labeled "socially maladjusted or delinquent but not emotionally disturbed" because a loophole in the federal definition appeared to permit this.

When court decisions limited the authority of administrators to suspend or exclude students who had been granted special education services because of their special needs, some administrators refused to grant such special status to students they thought they might later wish to suspend. These and similar exclusionary behaviors are documented in the records of hearings into violations of the rights of individual students or testimony before legislative committees.

This history underlines the importance of moral self-examination by each of us as a responsible parent, teacher, or legislator. Rights we now take for granted were withheld for many years while courageous, clear-thinking women and men worked to educate each other and their fellow citizens about the meaning of the fundamental ethical principle of equality in a democracy.

The laws that have been passed to date represent efforts to codify that principle, but laws are clumsy tools at best, and local custom or prejudice may support efforts at evasion. Behavior can be legal even if unethical. C-o-m-p-l-i-c-a-t-e-d. How might an ethical educator behave? Too much self-righteousness is inappropriate. If we peer closely enough at our own habitual ways of behaving, we may find "blind spots" in the application of ethical principles or even laws to which we believe ourselves sincerely committed.

We may be justifying exclusion because we were unaware anyone was feeling excluded. Or, we may be demanding inclusion on the basis of principle when it is not in the best interests of an individual student. Many writers about the application of ethical principles to everyday living use the metaphor of rushing ahead only to trip on an unnoticed obstacle in the path or fall into a muddy pit. They challenge us to pick ourselves up and continue on our way, humbled but determined and full of hope. (personal communication, January 23, 2007)

Educational psychologist Mary Lee Enfield, PhD, states the following:

In my 50 years as an educator, I have seen major shifts in many areas of education. Two of the most significant have come in the areas of curriculum and attitude toward the struggling learner.

For the past 20 years, the language arts curriculum in our country's classrooms has basically left direct teaching of basic skills, which are foundational to higher levels of reading and written expression achievement. All children are expected to learn to read through an inductive/discovery process by "experiencing" language both written and verbal. A percentage of children can and do learn this way, but a large percentage do not.

This is supported by several sources, including the latest National Assessment of Educational Progress. In 2005, 87 percent of eighth-grade and 87 percent of fourth-grade African American students were below proficient in reading (proficient being defined as grade level), and 61 percent of eighth-grade and 59 percent of fourth-grade white students were below that level. In my judgment these data indicate a serious ethical dilemma in education. The majority of American children are not learning to read at an acceptable level.

The concept underlying No Child Left Behind (NCLB) legislation is excellent and highly ethical, but for a variety of reasons its implementation falls far short of its goal. I believe there is a crisis in the ethical standards of education regarding children who are "left behind." This group will enter the ranks of illiteracy and suffer the social and psychological consequences of their reading and writing inadequacies.

To make matters worse, there does not seem to be an equally serious concern on the part of those responsible. In fact, when pressed to account for these children's lack of progress, the "blame game" goes into high gear. Parents, ESL, poverty, etc., are blamed, and often the concern ends there. We as educators should be included and begin to see what we can do about it.

I also believe we have an ethical crisis in our attitudes toward these learners that has corroded a major reason for their lack of progress (i.e., a close examination and concentrated search for instruction that is compatible to their learning needs). These children need direct instruction in the basic skills of reading and writing. Environmental problems can and often do complicate their learning, but they need not preclude children from learning.

In my experience, removing direct, basic skill instruction from the language arts curriculum is an ethical issue. Without it an identifiable group of children are being deprived of acquiring lifelong skills in reading and written expression commensurate with their learning potential.

The curricula delivered in our classrooms across our country should be closely examined in relationship to the learner. If children are failing in one instructional method, it is our moral responsibility as educators to find the method(s) that best matches their learning needs. Compatible instruction can overcome and compensate for many environmental challenges in children's lives.

Every child can learn to read and write commensurate with their learning potential *if* they are taught in the way they learn best. (personal communication, January 23, 2007)

Ultimately a society benefits when its laws and school districts create policies and practices that from legal and educational perspectives set standards to best benefit students and families. Yet the effectiveness of law and policy depends as well on those hired to implement these laws and policies in daily school situations on behalf of real children, youth, and families. Thus, the individuals a district hires make a great deal of difference.

Aiming not only to select the best and the brightest applicants but also to employ candidates for all educational positions who are people of character determines how laws and curriculums bring benefit and hope to schools. This hope increases as schools employ ethical professionals who bring to the field their dedication and high standards to enhance their immediate work environment.

BEING THE TRUE YOU ON A JOB APPLICATION

When candidates awaiting an interview for an educational position come to a school building, they often feel anxious and under pressure. These aspiring educators realize that they are likely facing stiff competition for the job they so hope to land. Applicants sit in a school office waiting for the moment when their names will be called.

Inside the administrator's office, a team of interviewers, sometimes weary after a stretch of these conferences, sometimes stressed as they aim to discern the best person for the job, work together to decide the best fit for each position. These teams remain hopeful and excited to meet the person who will soon become a regular part of school life. What should they be looking for? How can they find that person?

Each team has an idea of the kind of person who would best fit the job it seeks to fill. Certainly personality counts. How candidates present themselves counts. Teams understand that an applicant feels a bit nervous. But, if the interviewers stay attuned to the ethical elements of their interviews, they will look beyond minor apparent nervousness or a person's apparel and sense genuineness, sincerity, and authenticity in addition to examining recommendations, capability, and college performance.

The job candidate who walks into the office must not only be real but also present genuine and accurate credentials and an honest application. Patty Hoge, HR coordinator for Bloomington Public Schools in Minnesota, responded to the following questions relative to the job application process and how ethics plays a part.

What areas of information in a job application are addressed and must be absolutely true?

- Work history—including the applicant's responsibilities and reason for leaving.
- Educational background—We require transcripts; they can be copies with the application but must be official when hired.
- Criminal history, which includes anything more serious than a traffic ticket. We do criminal background checks on all new hires. If we find that a candidate has not been truthful on the application, we withdraw the job offer.
- Three professional references.
- Applicants must sign the application, stating that all information given is true to the best of their knowledge.

When candidates are in an interview, what kinds of untrue information could they "fudge" or try to pass off to the team to make themselves look better?

- Overstating their level of responsibility and/or knowledge. Overstating their competence in technology.

How does the team try to sift out the "real person" in an interview?

- We include questions such as asking a candidate to share specific improvements they have brought to former employers and questions regarding core values. Part of putting together a good team is to include people that have a track record for reading people correctly. (There are truly those people who can get a read on a candidate within 10 minutes.) Skills that you develop in interviewing are reading body language, watching eye contact, and looking out for the "professional candidate."

Being human, it could happen that the team members do not detect aspects of a person that, if they knew the candidate, would make them choose to not hire the person. What occurs as a result of someone like that "slipping through" and getting hired?

- A good supervisor will start documenting problems immediately and put the employee on an improvement program. The sooner the process is started, and the more consistency there is in the follow-up, the easier it will be to terminate an employee if that is ultimately what needs to happen. (personal communication, January 29, 2007)

BEING YOURSELF DURING THE JOB INTERVIEW

When sitting at the table and facing the team, you have no one else but yourself to present. So who is that person? The job candidate that is you certainly presents a compilation of grades, a preservice record, and the words of previous employers and professors. But that person is also the individual who in essence felt the call to become an educator.

The dream of working with young people should certainly supersede what is in the application materials. As an aspiring educator, being deeply interested in obtaining the job in order to help young people, your true attitude cannot be hidden. Having come through school as a young person or having left the corporate world to find fuller career meaning in education, your journey is proof that your quest goes beyond staying with it simply to have summers off.

Thus, with your "heart in the right place" and your credentials in order, making eye contact and remembering to smile, your interview begins and progresses in as natural a manner as possible. You have a few laughs with the team, and you speak seriously of the lives of youth today. When things are ready to wrap up, you thank the school team for the opportunity to interview, express your desire to work in the position you have been seeking, shake hands, and walk out the door.

You breathe a sigh of relief, probably think about what you should have said but didn't during some parts of the conversation, and go on your way to await that important phone call. You believe that the interviewers met the real you, a person with a heart for young people, who wants to serve society by giving your level best in the field of education.

CHOOSING A CANDIDATE

Meanwhile back in the office, the interview team takes 15 minutes to debrief. The members of the team either grab a cup of coffee or get a drink of water. They reach for an energy bar or piece of chocolate in hopes of staying the course during a long day of interviewing. In addition, they weigh their impressions internally and verbally. They talk about you. They compare you with others they have interviewed. They file away their thoughts mentally and note some ideas to help them in their ultimate decision.

What kind of person is the team looking for? Certainly this varies by position and location. Yet, the common denominator of each team is a search for who is best. What is best beyond a stunning portfolio? Your best, not only in background, performance, and character, is you, the fullness of your potential. This includes the ethical and authentic you.

AN EDUCATOR OF CHARACTER

What is character in education? Consider that a person of character is one who, within the context of her humanity, allows for mistakes and restarts, seeking to do right by students, families, and colleagues. When expected to fulfill an obligation, she makes an effort to do so. When faced with complex circumstances, such an educator seeks to sort out what really matters and to prioritize the elements of an event so that she can engage in the process of assistance in the order of optimal kindness and effectiveness.

Bearing this in mind, how would an interview team learn about a candidate for a job? Certainly in an interview, situational questions are presented to enable the team to learn how a potential employee might handle a situation. At least the candidate can tell the team what he thinks should be done. However, when placed in an actual situation, under the pressure of reality, a person reacts based on who he truly is. When in a classroom crisis, training and character blend to determine the most ethical and most appropriate response to the situation.

An interview is like a rehearsal. Preservice teaching is like a rehearsal. An administrative internship is like a rehearsal. But in each of these instances, individuals respond in a setting for which they are not totally responsible. Thus, once the candidate officially takes a job, do true colors emerge? Well, maybe in seeking tenure this new hire must not allow his guard to go down. But, then what happens after he earns tenure?

If the full-fledged educational professional is on board, can the guard then come down? If it does come down, what person is there? Who is the real educator? Hopefully the real person is a person of integrity, an ethical educational professional. This professional is consistent throughout circumstances that he faces. He shows consistent care, respect, and honesty to people. An ethical educator shows fairness to others based on the greatest good for all involved.

INTEGRITY—BEING ETHICAL IN EDUCATIONAL WORK AND EVERYWHERE YOU GO

While you wait by the phone, the interviewers double-check that they have read through the files. They search their own minds and hearts and note their instincts as they work to select persons of honor. They discuss and they disagree. They discuss some "what ifs," and when all is said and done, they decide that you are the person they want to hire.

(If you have worked for some years now, try to recall how you found out you were hired. Was it a letter or a phone call? Maybe you cannot even remember at this point, but what an honor it was for a team to decide that you were the best person for the position!)

The phone rings. The administrator who led your interview congratulates you and invites you to an informal meeting with the staff at the school where you will be working. You go to the school on the specified day and time. Who arrives? It is only one person—the real you. Open, enthused, confident, a little nervous, hopeful, and ready to become part of this school community. In this community you will have the opportunity to interact with many students, families, and coworkers. In these exchanges, the real you, authentic and ethical, seeking to reach your full potential, embarks on a career in education.

CHARACTER AND PROFESSIONALISM

What motivates people to interview for an educational position, and once they are hired to stay there? How will their character interface with ethics and professionalism?

University of St. Thomas graduate student Bryan Haffey formerly taught theology (morality and social justice) to high school sophomores. As part of his undergraduate degree in philosophy, Bryan wrote a paper on ethics and offers the following perspective from these experiences.

When discussing the problem of ethics in teaching, we are looking at something very different from the problem of ethics in the practice of law, or politics, or business. I do believe that most teachers go into education for noble reasons. It would be absurd for them not to. Teachers (and I am referring specifically to K–12 educators), consistently have to deal with students who are often unmotivated, difficult parents, and administrators that are pulled in numerous directions.

Teachers are the first to be blamed if a child doesn't perform well in school or drops out or in some other way fails. The pay is lousy and the job is far from prestigious: "Those who can do, and those who can't teach." These are professionals who are rarely looked upon as professionals despite their education level.

As a whole, teachers teach because they believe in what they do. Where this inspiration comes from will undoubtedly vary from individual to individual. Certainly we could observe that teachers at Catholic and other religiously affiliated schools have their reasons for taking pay cuts to teach where they do.

Teachers who choose to work in underprivileged schools may or may not share those same reasons, though they do, without question, have reasons of their own. I believe that most people who go into teaching see their jobs as fitting into some more comprehensive view of the world that requires them to help and care for others.

The problem of ethics in teaching then is not so much an issue of deceit, theft, backbiting, and any other trite descriptions used to characterize other careers. There's not a lot of room for self-aggrandizement. We have certainly seen from time to time an issue of sexual abuse, though this is certainly far more an exception than a rule.

The biggest ethical problems in education (strictly among teachers, not administrators) are a lack of motivation and a lack of professionalism. The first carries its own punishments. Students are far more honest than most adults. If a teacher doesn't care, the students won't either. They will usually take advantage of the situation and attempt to use classroom time to engage in activities unrelated to their course, whether it be working on homework for another class or talking about what's going on next Friday.

Conversely, if an unmotivated teacher wants control, the classroom can quickly become an oppressive environment for all those involved. Students perform best for teachers they respect, and they will respect their teacher only if they know that he or she genuinely cares about them. If a teacher lacks this concern, the teacher's life can become hellish quickly. No matter what a résumé says, most students can spot a fraud a mile away.

The issue of professionalism is a little more tricky. If an individual in the corporate world has an MBA, they are respected by the society at large as being well established. They are hot commodities, and they are, without question, professionals. Individuals in the field of law are indisputably considered to be professionals.

If someone in the field of education gets an MEd or even a doctorate in education, however, they are still looked on as those who got an easy job because they couldn't cut it elsewhere by a large segment of the population (despite the fact that they are better educated than the majority of that population). It is easy for these views to be absorbed by educators, and insofar as they do so, there can be a real temptation to not take their job as seriously as they would any other field.

Teachers must recognize the serious responsibility they have to their students and thus the responsibility they have to be a true professional. This includes the most basic elements of showing up to class on time, treating students and their parents with respect, and dressing like a professional.

In addition, the teachers must be committed to developing themselves as teachers. This includes an effort to constantly broaden the knowledge they have of their subject and a dedication to developing their understanding of how to convey the information they possess. There's no reason teachers shouldn't make a point of taking additional classes themselves, joining professional organizations, and attending education conferences. This is what professionals do. Students and parents will take teachers as seriously as they take themselves. (personal communication, January 17, 2007)

Ethics and professionalism blend intricately as educators express themselves in the workplace. The more ethical and the more professional the individual, the greater likelihood that her service to a school system is optimal and that she does what is right for the benefit of the individuals that she serves.

DOING THE RIGHT THING

As the days on the job pass, many circumstances will occur. You will determine how to relate with a variety of people. You will make judgment calls. You will meet challenges and find opportunities to rise to the occasion and respond to sudden crises. You will experience events that will seem insignificant but that require you to respond with a phrase or sentence that will determine the tomorrows of children.

An expression on your face could bring a colleague through the next hour, or by ignoring this coworker, unbeknownst to you, you could reinforce his sense of defeat. You may be asked to tell a parent something that is not true about what the school is doing for her child. You may notice something about a young person that puts you in the delicate position of seeking help for a family. Many events will bring you to the point of responding as you, the real, most authentic, and ethical you.

How will you know you are doing the right thing as you face the many choices and decisions that confront you and your colleagues each day? Since there is no way to predict how one would conduct themselves, consider that principles and general guidelines that you bear within your mind and heart will be there to govern your actions when you go to work each day.

Tom Burnett, a passenger on United Airlines Flight 93, had to act quickly on his principles when he and other passengers took over the plane that ultimately crashed in a Pennsylvania field on September 11, 2001. He had little time to analyze his situation. He did what he did based on the person he was when he got on the plane that morning. Like teachers who go to work each day, Tom was going to work as he was. His actions on Flight 93 made him a hero.

Tom's wife, Deena Burnett (2006), explains—based on her husband's actions—what brings a person to do what is right in the various circumstances of life. She states:

> If Tom were alive today he'd laugh at the idea of being called a hero. He would tell you he was just doing the right thing.
>
> Many today believe that there is no absolute right or wrong. If this were true, then we would have no heroes. Our concept of the word "hero" contains within it the assumption that this individual has chosen to do the right thing in difficult circumstances. It is precisely the accomplishment of this right thing at the right moment, which had earned the individual the title of hero.
>
> Implied then is that in a given set of circumstances there is a right thing to do. This means right and wrong are not relative. What seems right for you is not right for just you and what seems right to me is not right for just me. There are some things that *are* right and some that *are* wrong.
>
> I believe each of us in the core of our being knows what these things are. For instance, we would never call one who has murdered in anger or for selfish reasons a hero. Yet we would call someone a hero who has killed in order to protect others. We know that what the Nazis did to the Jews during World War II was wrong. However, when the Allies stormed the concentration camps killing the Germans, we can all agree that this aided them in setting innocent captives free, which is right.
>
> It is not that the passengers of Fight 93 took random action on September 11, 2001, which made them heroes, but that in our eyes, they did the right thing. Going forward, this is what each of us must seek to do everyday in our interactions. The right thing at the right time. Knowing it. Doing it.
>
> Looked at another way, how could we hope to make good decisions if there was no absolute right and wrong? Against what standard could we

weight both sides in order to determine what was best, so we could move forward in confidence and conviction, ready to stand our ground, and even fight if it became necessary? What if during the 1930s and 1940s we had said, it may not be what we would do, but if it's what Hitler wants, then we're okay with that? Where would our world be today?

If we are to have a future, we must determine that which is absolutely right and do whatever we can to move its cause forward and protect it, just like the passengers of Flight 93. Just like Tom. (pp. 89, 90)

What are your principles now, and how will they help you in education? Whatever they are, that is what comes with you to school each day. For example, if you believe that all persons have value and deserve to be treated with respect, then no second-class students will spend their days in your classroom and no families of lesser importance will come to your office with concerns.

If you believe that honesty is an important principle, you will grade students accurately no matter what position their parents have in the community. If you believe everyone should reach his or her full potential, then when you discover that a child could benefit from certain educational options or outside services, you will work so that he or she receives that opportunity. If you believe in the dignity of others, you will work to help maintain that dignity by keeping a student's struggles and family matters confidential.

Social workers, when receiving their professional training, learn about the ethics of confidentiality. When asked how social work training and the perspective and mind-set of a social worker would benefit a teacher, Sandi Lindgren, LICSW of Minneapolis, offers perspective. Her work, both as a school social worker and as an outside therapist, brought her to insights relative to educational ethics as follows:

1. Confidentiality: Respecting personal information is a part of social work training. It is important that a parent be consulted before a child speaks with a social worker.
2. Mandated reporters: There is need for more growth and explicit training for teachers in the area of sexual abuse and reporting suspected abuse.
3. Boundaries: Social workers have a clear sense of boundaries between themselves and clients, but the clarity of these lines between students

and teachers is less clear. Students sometimes know personal information about their teachers such as where they live. This kind of relationship needs to be examined and clarified for conscious decision
making. Going on a home visit has its boundaries as well. One should
never go alone to the home of a student.

4. Conflict management and mediation skills: Consider that when a behavioral issue is escalating, some teachers believe that students
   should work it out themselves. Some staff will let it go, figuring that
   someone else will deal with it. Ethically any behavior problem must
   be addressed to ensure school safety and enhanced learning.

5. Discussion of students: Sometimes teachers discuss a particular student among themselves when they are within range of other students.
   Also, a teacher may discuss one student in front of other students and
   thus break confidentiality. For example, "Tommy is also dealing with
   your issues." (personal communication, October 13, 2006)

Social workers have much to teach others in education about the value
of confidentiality and responsibility for addressing important situations
involving abuse and student behavior. Individual understanding of
what it means to be an ethical educator evolves and develops. The more
one learns and observes in coworkers, the more one can incorporate her
understandings into her own professional ethical behavior.

GIVING YOUR DISTRICT ITS DUE

Thinking back to Megan Post, we saw a teacher who was in special education primarily to earn the second income enabling her and her husband to take a winter trip each year. Megan showed up, and she taught
as was required by her contract. But did Megan give her heart to her
students and families? Did she put care and concern into this job, or
was her job simply a means to a personal end?

Certainly all staff enjoy earning money for a winter vacation. However, one can be excited about earning money to travel and still give his
heart to his work and give his school district its just due. What does the
district deserve from its employees? Consider these examples.

A district owns copy paper, pens, computers, and various other materials bought by taxpayer money for the purpose of running the school

on a day-to-day basis. Pilfering items for home use, though relatively minor, gradually depreciates the supply over time.

Borrowing district property for personal use without permission crosses a line as well. Taking home a laptop computer to surf the net as a means of evening entertainment is different from taking it home to develop new computer skills. Grabbing markers to make sale signs for the weekend garage sale stretches boundaries too.

Working the required hours matters. Habitual tardiness or leaving early just to leave early on a regular basis suggests that the job is not of prime importance and detracts from what the district expects. It can send the message as well that the staff person does not care about her position and professional duties.

What about sick days and "mental health" days? Does shopping at the mall for "mental health" justify calling a substitute? At what point is it important, when cold symptoms manifest themselves, to take a day to prevent things from evolving into pneumonia or spreading germs to others?

When the district holds a meeting of hundreds of staff in one central location and attendance is expected but not taken, would an ethical educator revert to the "they will never know the difference" mentality? Perhaps someone with such a mind-set looks to external parameters to determine personal behavior as opposed to having the character and an internal set of ethics.

Having character certainly points to giving the school district its due. Is it possible to give too much? What about your personal and family life? What about taking care of you?

GIVING YOUR DISTRICT "OVER ITS DUE"

While there are educators who give their district its just due, there are some who in a sense overdo it on the job and put the pressure on peers to do the same. Not all employed by a school can give the same exact effort and energy to their work in terms of staying past hours, volunteering for committees, or taking training for professional growth.

Some have very legitimate responsibilities on the home front with children and aging parents in the local community or far away. Others have pursuits that lend them the balance they need in order to maintain their professional lives effectively.

Thus is it ethical to press colleagues to become workaholics to a level that is not healthy for them? Perhaps one teacher is in a life stage that enables him or her to work long hours, create new and exciting units on a continuous basis, and regularly seek after-hours training and extra meetings. In the eyes of someone on the outside, those who find fulfillment and opportunity in placing high demands on themselves in their careers look as if they are doing the best jobs.

On the other hand, staff who are sincere, have a caring and positive attitude, and give each student, parent, and staff member their full presence while on the job should be given consideration. While still acknowledging that their first responsibility is their nuclear family or a friend dealing with a crisis, such professionals give of themselves. In so doing they live in an ethical manner relative to the whole picture.

They bring to their jobs a sense of decency and understanding for human need. Having this care and concern, they not only treat their family and friends with high regard but also give of their caring natures to those they serve and relate with in the educational environment.

Teachers of various types and personalities come to the job as mature adults who lead balanced lives. They aim to give their best while taking care of their personal priorities and lives so as to avoid burnout. Following are six S's, suggestions to maintain balance in order to maintain professional lives long term.

1. Sleep: Having adequate rest allows the educator to not only work efficiently and effectively on the job but also notice the nuances and see the students' lives and circumstances in context and in the moment. An alert educator can respond to crises, affirm students with appropriate comments suited to situations, and flexibly gear lessons to a range of students at a time.
2. Support: With a support system on the job and outside the educational world, teachers can run situations and ideas by confidants for perspective, affirmation, and encouragement. Whether it be a friend, counselor, relative, pastor, or small group set up for a specific kind of support, this help is an asset. Those on the job who reach out to help others gain assistance for themselves as well.

3. Spirituality: This varies among educators and takes the form of religion, recovery programs, prayer, spending time in natural settings, and reading inspirational material. It may mean having a mind-set of seeing grace and wisdom on the job or outside the workplace. Altruistic motives for assisting families, supporting colleagues, and teaching young people bring meaning into the lives of educators seeking to improve their particular spheres of influence.

4. Strength training/exercise/diet: Healthy habits benefit those who value themselves enough to take care of their bodies. Regular exercise, whether at a club or outdoors, gives the body strength and endurance. Eating food to enhance health provides an edge on the job. Seeking the advice of a trainer or health expert helps each individual find the level of activity and the foods best suited for her. The result—more energy and stamina to bring to the job and to life in general.

5. Sabbath time: Taking time off from work may mean that which is religiously prescribed for some or personally chosen for others. Working and pushing ahead at a constant speed do not offer time for relaxation and rest. The body, mind, and spirit find refreshment in alternative activities such as gatherings with people for fun, hobbies, and pursuit of the arts. Renewal comes from doing as the word specifies—finding new activities and new experiences again and again.

6. Solitude: School is a busy place. The opposite, downtime and solo time, brings balance. The educator who takes the opportunity to make a weekend retreat, or head out of town to go fishing, finds peace and perspective. Once reconnected with his inner life—which emerges in an environment without distraction—new ideas, goals, and solutions to everyday concerns surface more readily. Time away helps gain richness to bring back to enhance experiences with others.

Though some find satisfaction in putting all their energy into their school lives, others find fulfillment through variety. Wherever an educator puts focus for the moment, the important thing about it is the quality of that presence. Ethical educators are able to review the big

picture of life, both professional and personal, and live it in a manner
that is respectful to others as well as to themselves.

GIVING COLLEAGUES CREDIT WHERE CREDIT IS DUE

Working in close proximity with one another, it is common for teachers and other staff to exchange ideas and to develop lessons, projects,
and plans together. During such exchanges the line between who contributed or thought of a certain idea becomes blurred. In this case, when
success occurs, who claims the credit?

For instance, suppose a group of social studies teachers develops a
unit on local history that includes a reenactment of an exchange between two individuals who began the first log school in the county.
Then consider that a photo of that reenactment gets into the local newspaper. In addition, suppose that the teacher who was photographed and
interviewed with the students reenacting the event was one of the team
who developed the history unit but was not the one who designed the
featured lesson.

The teacher in the photo mentions in the interview that she worked
hard putting this together with her class, how much they enjoyed what
they learned, and so on, but failed to credit the teacher who actually
spent long hours on the lesson used. Feeling left out yet uncomfortable
about saying anything so as not to look like a "glory hound," the
teacher who was entitled to credit chose to say nothing.

Eventually team trust wore down. The teacher in the photo received a nomination for a community award due to her "efforts."
How easy it would have been to give credit to the other teacher, in
fact to the entire team that had developed the unit. Will you who have
been recently hired find that teachers have a hard time crediting one
another? Does the need for personal praise cloud staff ability to give
praise for professional success? What needs to happen to increase this
comfort?

Perhaps teachers need to begin with simple affirmations to one another during the school day. Educators praise students readily. Can they
praise one another as well? Following are five examples of affirmations
that staff can offer one another:

1. "Last night at the supermarket I overheard two parents speak about your good rapport with students."
2. "Since you joined our team, we have become more creative."
3. "When I passed your classroom yesterday, the students seemed so engaged in their experiments."
4. "The students from special education seem to be very comfortable in your classroom."
5. "When we discuss student behavior I can always depend upon you to share an effective solution."

A few words spoken with sincerity bring to the school environment an atmosphere of positive communication. When staff members feel comfortable praising one another, the likelihood for unethical behavior diminishes. Educators who feel comfortable praising colleagues in the small things can certainly bring them on board to share mutual successes as well.

YOUR WORDS AT SCHOOL AND IN THE COMMUNITY

Speaking to students, colleagues, and families is a continual part of the day of any educator. The tone of voice, the eye contact, the manner of approach, and speech content communicate to everyone interacting with staff. Whether with the "big people" or the "little people," those of mature years or young age, those of high status in the system or those in jobs perceived to be of lesser status, what you say and how you say it matters.

Where do ethics and integrity come in, then? It begins with choosing to give all people in the school environment the dignity they deserve simply due to the fact that they are human beings. Educators not only model mature and appropriate behavior or immature and inappropriate behavior to students, these adults in positions of influence also have a unique responsibility because of such positions. Children mimic adults. They copy adult walk, talk, ideas, and values.

Simply speaking respectfully to others in a school environment speaks volumes to students. When students witness adult educators speaking with respect to others, they learn that this is the way to treat others. Consequently, consistent respectful adult behavior is ethical behavior because it is part of the teaching and learning process imparted to young people.

When adult educators make a mistake and apologize to students or other staff, they are showing students the proper way to end conflict. When adult educators forgive the wrongs of students and staff, they model reconciliation. Thus by being respectful and forgiving in their dealings with the young and with their peers, ethical adult educators bear in mind that they are the lesson in how to relate to others in the school environment.

When staff members gather in the teachers lounge, it is easy to let down their guard and begin to blow off steam about students and parents. Sometimes the conversations begin in search of understanding and sympathy. Sometimes complaints are an effort on the part of teachers to relieve stress.

Yet, teachers and other school personnel must remember that their words, once spoken in public, cannot be retracted. Discussion of private information about students and families does not belong in a teachers lounge for all to hear any more than does any educator's private information given to a doctor belong in the waiting room of a clinic.

Part of being a new or seasoned professional is allowing people to trust you with their lives and their dreams, hopes, successes, secrets, failures, and private situations. When they make the step to trust staff with this, they are not only asking for your support and help but also asking you to be part of their hearts. Your observations and understandings, whether indirectly noticed or shared directly with you, are part of the bond of trust.

Whether you have an educational opinion or a report from an outside psychologist, the information belongs in proper context and in an appropriate environment. This information belongs with a team seeking to help a student and family, not within a group interested in the lives of others for mere entertainment.

The discussion of private information has a place and a time. An ethical educator knows where and when to discuss these matters, and it is not in the staff lounge. (For more on managing lounge conversations, see *Surviving Internal Politics within the School*, by Johns, McGrath, and Mathur [2006], chapter 3, "Surviving the Teachers Lounge.")

As with the story of Megan Post, it is clear that one slip can send a negative ripple into the community at large. A single slip of the tongue in the wrong place, at the wrong time, for the wrong reasons can create a poor image for a school, a staff person, or a building program or project. A negative message about a student or a comment private in nature could bring sadness, mistrust, or hurt to the fore in the mind and heart of an otherwise respectful and supportive member of the public or even a parent.

Were a psychiatrist, lawyer, or clergyperson to speak as offhandedly as Megan Post did, the ramifications would be very negative. Educators who put themselves into the category of nonprofessionals speak freely about school matters, district issues, and classroom occurrences with no thought of the effects of their words. Educators who consider themselves professionals use discernment before speaking about private school matters.

These ethical professionals consider to whom they are speaking, the content of their speech, and the potential of their words to offend or alienate those with whom they work daily. Ethical educators consider the impact of their words and actions upon those they may meet in the future and those whose dignity depends upon their discretion.

When an employee is out in public, he represents the organization that hired him after that first interview. Even if a teacher is dressing in Saturday casuals or a principal is lunching at a café in another state during spring break, both risk the possibility of a person they know or a person who recognizes them as an educator observing their actions or overhearing their words. Doing damage to the school district, families, a student, or the education profession in general is not worth the relief of frustration it gives to those having the conversation.

The trust you receive from the community is too important to lose as it takes time to build and to cultivate. In some respects you are an educator 24/7 and should bear that in mind wherever engaging in school talk. Having appropriate confidential persons and places for job-related matters is the professional and ethical thing to do.

SUMMARY

The effective implementation of school policy over time is determined by whom a district hires. Those teams who select an educator of character enhance their school climate. There are varied ways that educators express their ethical standards and perspectives in a school environment for the betterment of their coworkers, students, and themselves.

REFERENCES

Burnett, D. 2006. *Fighting back*. Longwood, FL: Advantage Books.
Johns, B., McGrath, M., and Mathur, S. 2006. *Surviving internal politics within the school*. Lanham, MD: Rowman & Littlefield Education.

CHAPTER 3

Everyday Challenges to Our Educational Values

Principal Max Finnegan looked out of his office window at the green hills in the distance. He greatly anticipated that future day when he would become a school superintendent. In the meantime, he had to rise in the organization in the proper way. He would work as a principal in a few schools so that his résumé reflected variety. Perhaps after a few years as an elementary principal, some as a secondary principal, he could become an assistant superintendent.

Max enjoyed daydreaming about reaching this goal. His classmate in graduate school, Pat Reasoner, had the same aspirations. But Pat had a whole different attitude that Max thought could drag his buddy down. Pat seemed to have more feeling about the whole thing and talked often of spending time with teachers and supporting families. This was not the way Max would go about it. He had his plan for the fast track to the top, and detours in the realm of deep involvement with his building staff, students, and families were not a part of that.

Instead Max thought that his time would be well spent by getting his name out to the right people. Knowing people on the top was very important. When Max attended committee meetings and worked on boards, he made sure that he drew the attention of the right people for his achievements. It seemed funny to Max that Pat would talk about being on boards and committees, too. But Pat actually seemed to do it for the sake of doing it. This seemed odd to Max. Why get so involved in a mere step to the prize?

Pat had expressed the dream of being a superintendent and how he wanted to impact the lives of many students and families. Max nodded and smiled. He had his own motives and methods for moving ahead. Max would make sure he was out of the building to get where he needed to go. A January conference in Orlando fit the bill. Then there was Pat, going to a leadership conference in Phoenix in July when he could be at his lake cabin. To Max, Pat had no strategic sense.

One strategy Max did know was that test scores would be part of his personal résumé. He was determined that his staff knew how to teach their students in a way that reflected well on their tests. When these scores came out in the newspaper, it was as good as seeing his name in print, favorably or unfavorably. Would he ever have the nerve to doctor the scores? This was something that would require a great deal of thought and planning. It would be just his luck to have a staff member be uncooperative at the wrong time.

That new teacher, Jill Akin, bothered him. She seemed to be a combination of a teacher who did things by the book and followed a higher calling of some kind. Jill had what appeared to be a real heart for her new career. Unfortunately she was one of the teachers working in a grade that had to be tested.

Would a young teacher just out of college have the nerve to challenge his way of doing things? Time would tell. Perhaps he would have to study her to find a weakness so he would know how to gain the upper hand. There must be some way to intimidate her. In time he would find her Achilles' heel, and then he could get her to go in his direction for sure.

Yes, school superintendent was definitely his endgame. Ms. Jensen, the administrative assistant, interrupted Max's thoughts. Pat Reasoner was on the phone. Would he like to work with him on a project for their current class at the university? Pat was thinking that educational ethics might be an interesting topic to pursue.

WANTING TO ADVANCE WHILE TREATING COLLEAGUES IN AN ETHICAL MANNER

Some educators find satisfaction in their jobs, making meaning in the daily events of typical school life. Others seek to work in various roles, finding meaning in variety. Some desire to move to higher paying positions for various reasons. Some know they have a sincere passion for making changes, influencing many, and participating in the big picture of education. Coupled with that they also know they need to support their families with competitive income and appropriate earning power.

They combine their altruism with realistic financial planning and proceed into their careers aiming to achieve these ends. Their genuineness propels them forward to the advanced positions and situations they seek. Various educators determine to work in different types of educational positions, searching for career fulfillment with little external advancement and prestige or with clearly defined goals for monetary and positional progression. Such individuals work in schools in very ethical ways, and others operate in less ethical ways.

For example, some choose to stay put for decades and employ manipulation and subtle power plays to govern the hallways they choose to dominate. Others climb over anyone to reach what they perceive to be the top. If that means representing others dishonestly, intimidating those of a quieter nature, or ingratiating the right people, they move forward full steam ahead. Personal relationships, genuine interest in others, and sincerity go by the wayside as being deterrents to the big job or the top spot, at least as they perceive it.

One way that educators block their peers so they themselves can get ahead is to know the circumstances of others and set up the stage so they alone are sure to shine. For instance, some teachers have young children and other family obligations that require them to leave at a certain time of the day. On the other hand, some have more time and less home responsibility and choose to make school the center of their lives. In doing so they arrange for after-school committee meetings and events, where they can be perceived as the "star."

In inviting other staff to take part, they then set up their peers for an instant downward plunge in the eyes of administration. Since they know full well that due to day care or an aging parent, peers will not be able to participate, these rising "stars" have a surefire chance to shine. Unable to participate, peers are made to appear less dedicated. In this way, the spotlight will shine brightly on only one or a few who have staged this unethically arranged professional showcasing.

Pretending sympathy for those unable to participate, such teachers then smile knowingly at administration, certain that they are noticed and seen as doing what is right in the current circumstances. Experiences such as these become cumulative. These individuals, lacking personal ethics, then determine the philosophy of the principal and make sure to know as much as they can about methods and events that support the thinking of administration, regardless of their own personal preferences.

Looking out for students is way off their radar screen. To become lackeys of the boss means an easier road, a favored status, and a better position in the eyes of those in the upper echelons.

Certainly there is nothing wrong with wanting to be recognized and acknowledged for one's achievements. Everyone wants to be affirmed, noticed, and included in an organization. However, the previous dynamics speak of being ruthless, dishonest, and manipulative. An ethical educator works for the goal of helping others, appreciates genuine praise, gives recognition where it is due, speaks forthrightly about her educational beliefs, and respects those of others.

An ethical educator is sensitive to the personal commitments of peers and works to bring everyone on board through thoughtfulness, flexibility, and consensus. Ethical educators shine when they seek to bring about circumstances that open doors for others. They are inclusive and receptive as they powerfully demonstrate their ethical professionalism.

WANTING TO BE RECOGNIZED WHILE TREATING STUDENTS ETHICALLY

Serving on committees and attending conferences help educators develop and grow professionally. Ultimately, contributions to education outside of the school and participation in conferences make a teacher or administrator more competent and adept at what he does. This certainly benefits the school community.

Sometimes, though, outside involvement robs the immediate and primary position of the educator. Extensive absences deprive classrooms and faculties of the instruction, understanding, and leadership so necessary on a consistent basis. When a teacher or administrator is gone too much, relationships suffer. Students who require stability and consistency lose out. Teachers who need administrative support and advice flounder without the necessary and easily accessible perspective of principals and directors.

Though outside involvement of staff members is certainly beneficial to buildings, those who leave must also do their best to take consistent care of their own backyards. Success outside of school cannot cover for failure "at home." An ethical educator knows how to strike the right balance between "tending her own gardens" and working in the larger arena of education.

When around the same students, day in and day out, teachers know how to recognize the struggles and successes of these young people. Such teachers know what to say and how to redirect students toward their optimal performance. As capable as reserve teachers certainly are, they are unable to forge short term the kind of close relationships that exist between students and their "real" teacher.

When a crisis occurs, an assigned stand-in staff member may not be the best person to handle it, especially if the principal has established trust with a student or family. Though it is hard to be all things to all people, right priorities and balanced planning enable teachers and administrators to be on deck for most circumstances. Though gone on occasion, if teachers and administrators have kept in step with students and staff, it is not difficult to regain rapport and read the difficulties that have evolved during an absence.

Teachers and principals who stay close with students know who among their charges are the most vulnerable. Until some students are able to fend for themselves against the class bully or meet the confusion of a large building comfortably, these young people benefit best from the presence of those they trust. Insightful adults know when to lend a hand, arrange for a student's comfort in the environment, and steer away trouble.

These educators risk standing up for the "little guy," whether that would be students who are intellectually and socially vulnerable, ethnically and racially in a minority, or physically and economically at a disadvantage. Serving as guardians for those at risk does not earn status in the community and large-scale national recognition.

Doing small things daily and consistently to keep students operating successfully and functioning capably and safely does not make the front page. It may not even merit an impressive present at the end of the year, yet for the ethical educator, such actions are the only right way to operate to ensure student success.

Ethical educators also realize that each student is a unique individual, with unique learning, social, and emotional needs. Some require little attention, work well independently, and prefer lesser involvement with an instructor. Others, however, come to class with "empty cups" that constantly need to be refilled. Teachers who know how to address individual student needs and balance the polarities presented by each group of young people they serve work artfully as well as ethically to help the range of students assigned to their classrooms.

While working with individual students, skilled educators know how to address their individual needs. They develop a repertoire of strategies and acquire a variety of skills in order to be able to attend to the academic and behavioral ranges of their students. When instructional trends come in and out of favor in education, wise educators separate what is solid from that which is ineffective, knowing that educational fads come and go in the marketplace of ideas.

Ethical educators are cautious about risking the educational future of their students on trendy programs, which though smartly packaged and well presented, could prove inappropriate, even lethal, for some of their students. Doing educational damage to even one student in the name of teaching according to current styles and fads is not what an ethical educator is about.

Speaking up on the behalf of the needs of all students and adjusting their 504 plans or individualized education programs (IEPs) accordingly is in the true nature of an ethical educator. Arranging for extra help, volunteer time, and educational options is the means to address student needs beyond the capability and time constraints of one person for the benefit of many.

Ethical educators make decisions to educationally serve their students. They make referrals and present students for special education based on student appropriateness for the opportunity. Such a teacher would not seek referrals to special education to ensure his caseload has sufficient student numbers to avoid transfer or bring in funds to a district. Referrals and placement decisions are made in good faith to benefit young people and their futures as opposed to adults and their present convenience, comfort level, and preferences.

FACING THE CHALLENGES OF COMMON ETHICAL DILEMMAS IN THE SCHOOLS

Sometimes school staff face ethical dilemmas and feel very alone. In order to emphasize that there are others out there who experience challenges and pressures in the area of ethics, some such occurrences will be mentioned and addressed.

Ethical Boundaries

Many ethical concerns fall in the area of boundaries. Teachers notice distress in students, link the distress to home situations, and wonder when and how to step in to help ease a student's burden. Sometimes these issues relate to parenting, family lifestyles, or even abuse. In minor matters, a brief call home relaying what has been observed in the demeanor and performance of the child may be a start.

Speaking respectfully and with understanding of the challenges parents face and how busy they are will help to open the subject of concern. If staff members suspect that the child needs psychological support, it may work to search this out gently with a parent at a conference or discuss the concerns with the building mental health staff or administrator. Together, appropriate staff members can determine the next step.

If a school employee has actually seen physical evidence of abuse, the school nurse or mental health staff often lend support in the reporting process, as this is a must. By nature of an educator's role, staff members are mandated reporters. It may happen that someone in administration or on staff who is also aware of the same situation will try for whatever reason to deter a reporter.

However, since withholding the reporting is not an option, and the opinion of another does not weigh in on what has been witnessed, the one who has the information must move forward in spite of criticism. If a child speaks to a school adult and hints at sexual abuse, it never hurts to ask the opinion of those working in child protection to determine if an incident is truly a reportable incident. This staffer may have other information that this next call may support or verify.

If the reporter is unable to enlist child protection involvement at one point, it may happen that a future incident will bring further clarity to the situation, enabling these trained professionals to come into the situation.

Being alert and willing to help will hopefully bring the assistance that is necessary in due course.

religion

Another ethical aspect of boundaries is in relationship to religion and politics. Though staff members have a range of religious and political beliefs and have a right to deep convictions in these areas, they have to watch how they present their opinions when students are involved. A teacher of the social sciences must present all viewpoints and remain objective. Whether they choose to share their political preferences may be their option, yet how this is done is the point.

When a teacher shares that she supports Jane Smith for the Senate and Joe Johnson for the House, she may explain this as an illustration of why she supports someone, while at the same time saying that the parents of the students may support them or their opponents and state their respect for the opinions of others.

Encouragement for all of age to vote takes priority over what opinion a staff person may have. Teachers may want to consider refraining from sharing their political biases and preferences so as not to compromise the objectivity of students. However, when a school board election is going on, schools do make public whom the union supports. Teachers also make it known what candidates say on educational issues that directly impact the school system.

When religion enters in, educators again may hold firm convictions. Their best representation of their own religious beliefs is their personal conduct. How school faculties treat students, families, and coworkers does primarily speak the message of their personal values. In some schools, teachers can wear emblems representative of their religions, but when they do so, they are in effect saying that their actions connect to their religions.

Thus, character is optimal if they care to positively identify with the group connected to the emblems around their necks or on their lapels. In some public schools, emblems depicting religion may not be allowed.

Students often ask teachers for advice. In many circumstances educators can give general advice acceptable across the board. However, when a student asks for direction on a matter that impacts his family and interfaces with his religious beliefs, a teacher is wise to encourage the young person to direct questions to someone in the appropriate domain, such as a pastor, family therapist, or wise community figure respected by his family.

Students trust teachers. Sometimes they have only a teacher to turn to for support, especially if they come from a fragile and challenged family. When a staff person senses she is on tender territory and faced with a topic that is sensitive, she would be wise to seek out someone in the district who has the legitimate position of assisting her in directing the student.

Students can be vulnerable. They are open to suggestion. An ardent teacher seeking to convert others does cross a line in the public school arena when seeking to persuade a student to say a certain prayer with him or to come to his place of worship to learn more about the religion the teacher holds with firm conviction.

What if a student attends a school affiliated with a religion? This is a whole different situation. Perhaps a child is not of the faith that runs a school but may be attending there due to the size, location, and moral climate of the school. In that case, the teachers and parents have to have an agreement as to the expectations relative to participation in religion classes, services, and prayers. Once this is clear there will be no surprises.

Even within a particular denomination there are varieties of expression. A teacher is wise to know the official teachings of the school's religious affiliation and to respect them. Whether they are members of the church themselves or not, respecting the doctrinal expression of the church school offers the students what their families have sent them there to learn. Confusing young people with personal opinion relative to that doctrine is not appropriate.

The bottom line: A young person admires and imitates character, kindness, ethics, and respectful behavior in adults. Every adult working in a school serves as a role model. Ethical educators know the value of working on their own manners, behavior, and relational skills. What they say and do becomes the message that supersedes any articulated political convictions and religious beliefs.

An ethical educator works to become a person of consistent character in the company of students, colleagues, and his own family and in the community. An ethical educator realizes that who she is the strongest message she can send to young people.

Respecting the Law and District Policy

When working in a school, teachers encounter various published material, some of which is copyrighted with specific directions. Other material comes with a statement of permission for copying for school use. It is important that educators know how to respect the laws of intellectual property and copyrights.

How does one begin in that regard? Some material is very straightforward, yet for other material there is a range of allowance for fair use depending on the circumstances. School districts have their own experts on these boundaries, and a staff member would be wise to check with the administrator, school resource librarian, curriculum expert, or technology director for current information. Lawyers working for a school district also know the law as it relates to school policy.

Many policy and legal challenges occur for educators. Perhaps a teacher, frustrated with a student's difficulties or pressured by parents, would so much like to get special help for a student. In the building where the teacher works, it has been made clear that the policy specifies that a teacher make a certain number of interventions before a child's cause is reviewed by a team. Once it appears to the team that such interventions are unsuccessful, a referral can then be made to special education for possible testing and qualification.

A teacher in this position who wants to expedite the process may be tempted to represent data in such a way that the child will pass easily through team consideration and into the referral process. Though the end is worthy, the means to that end do not follow policy.

Perhaps during the same season, a child in another teacher's class has needs as well, and the teacher involved has diligently documented data in order to present this child's cause to the team. Each child may deserve assistance, but basing help on correct data is the required and ethical thing to do. Patience and honesty will eventually lead to authentic assistance for a student.

Rigging is not right. Suppose a special education team is aware that the state department of education will be coming to review files. A teacher is pressured by his team leader to change dates on IEPs in order that the time span of assessment does not exceed a legal requirement. What happens if the teacher chooses to go against the grain? Being in the right regarding reporting, the special educator, who took a longer time to complete an assessment and hold a conference, chooses to keep the dates accurate.

The inspectors come, notice the time gaps, and suggest ways that the team might work within correct state guidelines. Being honest, although a challenge to the teacher, not only allows him to feel peace about his professional behavior but also helps the team become more efficient. Due to his stand, the likelihood is greater that ethics will determine the method of team operation for the future.

Knowing the law and district policies helps a staff person respond to unethical challenges made in the course of a workday. The more one knows, the less the chance of unwittingly becoming involved in unethical job behavior.

If an educator does not know the right direction, it would be wise to know whom to ask for clarification on any matter that potentially challenges one's sense of professional ethics. A former professor, a current director, local and state union personnel, and the state department of education would be resources to consult in order to maintain ethical professional practice.

When it comes to school law and educational policy, there are many considerations to be made by all employees of a school district. Dr. Janet Pladsen, assistant superintendent of academic affairs for Bloomington Public Schools in Minnesota, states:

> As educators, we are first and foremost role models for our students and for the community. Students place their trust in teachers, administrators, and staff members.
>
> There is an expectation that educators uphold the law and assure that the rights of the students are ensured in our schools. We are *in loco parentis*, the Latin term for "in the place of a parent." This refers to our legal responsibility as we take on some of the functions and responsibilities of a parent while we educate and care for the students during the instructional day. It is critical that educators understand their legal obligations and fulfill them to the greatest degree possible. (personal communication, February 12, 2007)

Systemic Ethics

Ethics become deeply embedded in any school system. A system takes on the characteristics of those who work within an organization.

Systemic ethics then come about as the result of the interface of government requirements, school district policy, and those who work to implement them.

Doing things in a particular way, an honest and legal way, is just how things are done in certain systems. When educational leaders move in a certain direction, staff members note the modeling and operate in accord with what they perceive as the way to function. Professionals often just do things in the flow of operation without giving thought to whether something is ethical or not. Often, going ahead with procedure and treating others in a respectful fashion just comes naturally as a positive system's power brings everyone along with it.

However, sometimes unethical habits gain the upper hand in schools and many educators go along, unconscious of the fact that they are performing their jobs in a way that is unethical. They move along with the idea that they are doing what is expected and typical in a school system. How then does it happen that a teacher or custodian or principal comes to understand that something is unethical?

Individuals with deep clarity regarding their personal ethical code know when they hit an event, request, or circumstance that asks them to break that code. It is engrained and emerges as needed. A well-formed conscience can be unrelenting when an individual is faced with the opportunity to speak the truth and act in an ethical manner.

An example of systemic issues that occur would be when an administrator places a new hire inappropriately. For instance, suppose a beginning school psychologist is assigned to a position that no one else in the department wants. Since this new employee lacks seniority, she has to take a job better suited for the capability of a more experienced person or a job in a school that has a challenging staff.

A more senior psychologist might be able to handle this just fine but does not feel like dealing with it. Consequently the new hire walks into a position that is politically way over her head. Signs of burnout become apparent after only three months. Since the system does allow such a placement in this location, it was right, but was it ethical?

To add another dimension to the dilemma described, what if several hardworking and busy staff persons who rejected the position, and due to seniority had the right to choose a more comfortable spot, see this new hire struggling and stressed and ignore what they see? If their passivity to the burnout they witness impacts this person's mental and physical health, does their indifference contribute to this beginner's professional decline? Would an "everyone for themselves" attitude in a school system be one to work to correct?

If so, do educational leaders have the courage and will to work to address practices that bring down those who would in more optimal and ethical circumstances offer a worthy contribution to education for years to come? If not, would those deemed as leaders remain indifferent to such occurrences and be content with this placement practice year after year?

Another example of embedded and habitual passive unethical behavior would be "passing the buck" instead of taking responsibility. For instance, if a staff person suspects a student is using drugs on a regular basis, even selling them, but does not want to take the time to verify this, thinking that certainly the teacher in the next period will pick up on the student's behavior, is such a teacher doing his job ethically?

Or, what if a teacher sees a student who could benefit from special education but is not up for filling out the forms? Maybe this teacher figures that someone else, like next year's teacher, will take up the cause. After all, does anyone ever ask about potential referrals? Administrative apathy engrained in a system trickles down to others, and consequently students fall through the cracks.

Further examples of teacher indifference that affect students would be writing reports that lack the detail necessary to actually express the reality of a student's performance. Teachers who believe they can cut corners think that no one will read these reports anyway so do not consider it is worth their time to pass on additional information. However, the omitted detail could be exactly what staff persons working with the student in the future need to know to better assist that young person.

Neglecting to call parents with praise of their child or constructive criticism that would help a parent do follow-up may be another omitted detail of a teacher's day that could make a big difference. Sometimes the decisions made on seemingly small matters and details could make a significant difference in the life of a child.

Another way that students suffer is due to teachers who acquiesce to common low-level behavior. Overlooking what they perceive to be bothersome and minor behaviors, such adults contribute to a building's lower standards. These annoying incidences, if allowed to continue, become the standard, the accepted, and the normative.

The indifference of staff to put-downs between students here and there, or some graffiti on a desk, or scraps on the floor contributes to negatively transforming a building in a direction that becomes acceptable. A compilation of low-level incidents brings a building in the opposite direction of its full potential as a respected and effective academic institution.

Sometimes schools tolerate the current culture instead of leading youth to a higher level of personal dignity. For example, a teacher required to chaperone a dance might feel very challenged witnessing provocative clothing and dancing when there is no administrative or parental backup or school policy to support interference of any kind. Left to hold the bag, the least the teacher may be able to do is to begin working with a small group of students who are also uncomfortable and begin to chip away over time at the big picture.

Staff Behavior

Sometimes a side of staff surfaces, starting with one person and then others follow. For example, if one teacher begins to gossip, it is easy for another and another and another to join in with them. Then before they know it, this group creates a circle where backstabbing is safe, habitual, and repetitive.

How easy it is to blow off steam about coworkers who are not carrying their load and to complain about such individuals, blaming them for making the jobs of others more difficult. Here at last is a place to grouse about administrators and complain about parents in a disrespectful manner.

But what does backstabbing do to an organization? Keith Hardy, Distinguished Toastmaster, community volunteer, and 2007 candidate for the St. Paul Board of Education, states the following:

> I have seen and felt the effects of backstabbing in a nonprofit organization. Backstabbing saps energy, whether you need to push yourself to not respond to it or you use valuable time refuting or fighting it. In our world, perception is tantamount to truth for some, so there is risk in not responding to backstabbing comments.

However, I have chosen what I consider a higher path. After years of fighting negative comments about me, I'm comfortable with my positive contributions to society and the knowledge that I aim for a positive life.

I know I make mistakes, and I am willing to apologize for them, to make amends where possible, and to acknowledge areas I can improve where appropriate.

Hence, if some people choose to waste time backstabbing me, I empathize with their loss of time for doing good, doing positive things for others, and I feel sorry for anyone who has to waste their valuable time listening to, reading, or otherwise entertaining the backstabbing comments.

I "confront" the backstabber by asking in what way have I offended them and what can I do to make amends. If no progress is made, I walk away and let them choose what's more important in the short time we have on Earth—speak negatively of Keith or spend time doing positive things for other people? (personal correspondence, February 12, 2007)

LEADING WITH PRINCIPLES

An individual who seeks to act in an ethical and consistent manner in all arenas of his or her life is known as having integrity. If educational leaders act with integrity, others in a school will more likely follow this example. Speaker and founder of the Business Revitalization Institute, Roxanne Emmerich (1999) asserts to leaders the importance of character in terms of influence on an organization: "To receive the trust of employees, you must lead with complete honesty. Trust is the solid foundation upon which the organization is built. To earn it there needs to be a strong commitment to truth." Emmerich further encourages leaders as follows: "Keep an open door—and an open mind. Rumors feed on ignorance. Truth warms the hearts of your people" (p. 27).

Another important component of leadership that impacts the entire school organization is respect. John C. Maxwell, PhD (2006), notes the following in regard to respect relative to emerging leaders. However this statement is worthy of note for all in education.

Respect is vital for leadership, yet it can be difficult to discern in young leaders who have not fully developed. Peer respect doesn't reveal ability, but it shows character. I have found the following acronym on respect a helpful device to evaluate the respectability of emerging leaders.

R = Respects their coworkers
E = Exceeds the expectations of others. Naturally sets the bar higher than anybody else sets it for them.
S = Stands firm on convictions and values.
P = Possesses maturity well beyond their years and shows self-confidence.
E = Experiences a healthy family life.
C = Contributes to the success of others.
T = Thinks ahead of the pack. Potential leaders are marked by their ability to outpace the thinking of those around them. (p. 23)

Respect does not come automatically with any leadership role. Victor Parachin (2006) offers the following as a law of leadership. "Remain balanced. Unfortunately some leaders operate with inflated egos. These types demand rather than command respect. No matter how high you rise or how important you become, remain a balanced person. Operate with a sense of humility" (p. 18).

Qualities such as lack of integrity and imbalance do occur among school leaders. Bob Knight, retired teacher, shares observations and perceptions of lack of ethics in educational leaders.

Three chief concerns would be:

1. Cloaking some educational change in the wording that it is "good for the children" when it, in fact, is based on economics or some other concern.
2. Compromising decision making (violating professed values) by taking the most expeditious path instead of the clearly morally correct one (consistent with professed values) because it is the easiest one (i.e., in order to placate some group).
3. Allowing the need for financial support to corrupt values (i.e., soda and junk food in the schools, recruiters—especially in low-income settings, for example). (personal communication, February 20, 2007)

Bonnie Bakkum Amundson, founder of Amundson Life Construction, offers workshops on ethical management of human behavior in the workplace. Her mission is to encourage a "workplace movement," creating communicative workplaces with common goals that everyone within the work environment (whatever that environment is) is willing to buy into. Here are Bonnie's seven suggestions for school principals:

1. You have a "position." Do it justice—don't lower your behavior. Make it a point to continue proving you are deserving of the position.
2. You are the principal, acting on principles, not on district politics.
3. If you have favorites among the staff, students, school board members . . . don't show it at work **and** don't share your thoughts on this subject with anyone who has any connection in your school system. Be fair.
4. You need to set the tempo. No backstabbing.
5. While you may be "in charge" don't ever lose sight of the fact that you are no closer to your God than anyone else. **Be strong enough to be humble.**
6. Recognize and practice giving positive feedback. We all need to know what we are doing right in order to keep doing it.
7. Be honest and do the RIGHT THING. After all, you are setting the standard. (interview with Amundson)

Comments from both a former teacher and an outside consultant challenge school leaders to be aware that others observe their actions. What a principal does and says sets the tone of a school. People are perceptive. Teachers, families, and students see how things happen. It is important that what they see is right and ethical on all counts.

Sometimes behaviors such as those listed have to be addressed. Unfortunately there are circumstances when a staff member has to confront ethical gaps in administration.

STANDING UP TO THE PRINCIPAL FOR YOUR PRINCIPLES

When building leaders abdicate from the role of ethical leadership and present teachers with a course of action that is not right, teachers may choose to take a stand. It may happen that a principal will be adamant on a curricular direction that differs from that of a teacher.

Such instances could include everything from the request to collude in a plan to doctor test scores or the insistence of an enthusiastic leader who just returned from a conference requesting teachers using a proven plan of instruction to switch on faith to another math method. What would be the best way for teachers to address the principal when they believe the direction requested is not ethical or the best option for students?

Following are five suggestions to consider when speaking with the building leader regarding challenging requests.

1. Maintain open channels of communication over all matters. If this is done and rapport is established between teacher and principal, it will be easier to present tougher topics.
2. Speak and act regularly with respect and integrity. When a staff person acts in accord with these principles, the principal will observe this manner of conduct. It would be much harder for a leader to ask someone who consistently adheres to ethical behavior to violate his principles than to ask someone who waffles on standards and has a minimal sense of moral correctness in the workplace.
3. Knowing the basis of ethical behavior and instructional practice helps one to stand firm when the time is right. Whether a teacher has strong beliefs regarding personal character or academic methods, the reason for a principle can be more easily articulated and expressed more naturally and positively.
4. Show courage of conviction, and be willing to enlist others to support a position or practice that has proved successful. When confronted by an educational leader, a teacher who has developed courage will be able to calmly and confidently explain why it matters to follow the law or district practice. Access to written information to reinforce a matter of contention will bring the facts into play and focus a dispute on data as opposed to what might be perceived as personal opinion.
5. Appeal to the dignity of the person offering the challenge. Pointing out the practice of ethics when it has been successful and recognized reinforces the desire in others to continue on the high road. Noting how staff, other educational leaders, and the community have developed respect for the way certain things have been done in a school encourages continuance of further ethical and successful practices.

SCHOOL POLICIES AND YOUR PRINCIPLES: WHICH IS HIGHER?

Sometimes school administrators or other staff persons experience challenges that place them "between the devil and the deep blue sea." Such circumstances pull individuals in two directions, where action may cause them to experience high risk no matter which choice is made.

What does an educator do when he or she has an inner conviction and moral assurance to act according to a higher law than that required by a school leader or that which is codified by law or policy? Such an educator may reach the point of placing conviction before the requirements of a job.

This could become an extremely difficult situation requiring the exposure of unethical behavior in the system, the potential loss of a job for insubordination, or the scorn of others who are willing to go along with the status quo. Whatever the case, taking the risk and following the determined high road will require a sense of moving forward in truth.

When an ethical educator acts according to such principles, he or she may for a time lose a position, a place in the building social structure, or approval of those who act within typical expectations at the school. One who moves forward on principle may experience loneliness, rejection, and defeat.

Yet if an educator acts on solid ground, the individual must move in the belief that she will again find that solid ground, whether it be in a position more suited to the standards upon which she has acted, among those who understand the reason for the action taken, or for the certainty that compromise of conviction was not an option.

Having moved forward upon principle, ultimately an educator of courage and ethical integrity knows personally the value of acting with honor. Thus such an educator has made a gain of the heart that cannot be lost regardless of external outcome.

SUMMARY

When educators enter a school system, they choose by their actions and character how they will make their way. Though the same persons will function within various educational arenas, their actions will be determined by their interior purposes and motives. Their external impact will be determined from their interior as well. Teachers will face decisions on how to respond to trendy programs and have to decide how to balance their time away from their school sites.

Those in education will have to determine their personal boundaries in terms of expressing their religious and political views so as to respect the lives of others and yet to also help them. No matter what educators do, consistent character will lead them toward actions that make them role models at all times while in the presence of students.

Teachers will face the question of getting services for students in an ethical manner or in a deceptive way. Educators will work in systems that perpetuate high or low standards. They will encounter embedded systemic unethical practices as well as passive indifference. When doing so they have to decide to go along or make their own way and face the consequences.

They will have to decide how to address backstabbing and realize that when they go a different way, they may be the subject of their peers' negative conversations. Teachers may encounter one-on-one conflict with the ethics of administration and may have to choose what appears to be a higher path. There is risk in being ethical, but the risk of refusing to act with integrity is greater in terms of damage to personal character.

REFERENCES

Emmerich, R. 1999. *Thank God it's Monday*. Minneapolis: Banner Books.
Maxwell, J. 2006. Picking potential leaders. *The Toastmaster* 72(9): 23.
Parachin, V. 2006. Laws for positive leadership: How to be a leader others want to follow. *The Toastmaster* 72(9): 18.

CHAPTER 4

Dealing with Conflicts of Interest

Beth is a bit apprehensive about her new position as a third-grade teacher at Jefferson Elementary School. Beth has taught for 15 years in another state, but her husband's job transfer has resulted in her position at Jefferson. Within the school community of Jefferson Elementary School, Beth finds 20 other teachers, a principal, a custodian, a school secretary, and 10 paraprofessionals. Beth prides herself in being ethical.

Her husband is in business, and she has heard some of the "horror stories" he has encountered; she has not been confronted with major issues within her profession. After her first week at Jefferson, she finds herself uncomfortable, but she can't pinpoint what is bothering her. Her colleagues seem to be friendly enough, but she decides to continue to observe and postpone any judgment.

One day at the copy machine, she notices a teacher copying flyers about an insurance forum. The teacher explains to Beth that she is selling insurance as a side job and invites Beth to come to the forum. A few minutes later, another teacher walks in and takes a call on his cell phone. She can't help but hear that he is arranging to leave school early to get to his other job.

Two days later, she is having lunch in the teachers lounge when another teacher walks in and proceeds to unload on Beth. "I am sick of Bill, Jane, and Margaret. They are so busy getting in good with the principal that they have forgotten about what is good for the kids." It seems that the teacher has just come from an IEP meeting where there was a discussion of special education placement. The three teachers had done nothing but complain about the child's behavior in class, in the lunchroom, and in the hall. However, when they got into the IEP meeting, they did not share any of the information because they were afraid of getting on the principal's bad side; the principal did not want the student placed in a special class.

About a week later, Beth is working late one day and the custodian comes into her class. In the process of collecting the trash, the custodian "unloads" on Beth, explaining that Jane is having an affair with the principal, and Jane gets many special privileges because of her involvement with the principal.

A few days later, one of Beth's students needs to go to another teacher's classroom to deliver a message to an older brother. Beth's students are currently in the lunchroom, so Beth walks her student to that classroom. When she arrives, she finds the teacher on the phone ordering some clothes from a clothing company while the students in the class do seat work. She notices that several students have their hands up with questions about their work. Beth is torn. What should she do—take her student back to lunch or stay here and help these students while the teacher talks on the phone?

A conflict has arisen for Beth—that conflict has been created because another teacher is using school time for personal use. Ethical violations seem to be "snowballing" in this school and are now creating problems for Beth, who is trying to do her job. As previously stated in chapter 1, ethical violations may start small and then get out of hand. Jefferson Elementary School has many problems, and those problems are indeed impacting the education of children. A climate of unethical behavior has been created, and it appears that many people there have become desensitized to it.

Beth has an immediate decision to make about what she should do and has a long-term decision to make about whether she wishes to stay when her contract is up in such a setting. Beth does know that she must remain ethical and should be mindful of everything she does so she does not fall into the unethical trap that has been created in this school.

Using school property or school time for personal use or to make money for another position are conflicts of interest that arise within the school setting. This chapter focuses on some of those issues and provides guidance on how to determine for what and how school property and time can be used.

The chapter also focuses on some other issues of conflict of interest that arise in the school setting. Educators don't always think of these issues as conflicts of interest, but they are. The chapter discusses the importance of disclosing potential conflicts of interest.

We must always remember that we are role models for our students. If we have other priorities, such as other positions, our students will hear the message that they are not our priority and we have other things to do than to teach them. While we all have other priorities, at school our priority is the children we serve. Within the school setting, the message we want to convey is that the children we teach are our priority. If we stop and reflect on what we are doing, we must always ask ourselves whether, while at school, we are putting the needs of our students first and foremost.

MOONLIGHTING—HAVING ANOTHER JOB

Because educators are not engaged in a well-paying profession and may have acquired significant loans to become teachers or are trying to support a family either as a single parent or in a two-parent household, they often find themselves in the position of having to moonlight to make a living that will support themselves and their families. Some educators have a second job in order to buy those extras that they couldn't purchase otherwise.

Moonlighting is certainly a reality in today's world. There isn't anything wrong with such a practice provided that the educator keeps the second job separate from the position as an educator.

What happens when the educator begins to blur the line between the second job and the teaching profession? The teacher is selling jewelry or baskets or insurance on the side. He or she has created a dilemma—the paperwork isn't getting done, so the teacher gives the children busy work to do within the classroom so he or she can catch up on the paperwork. Or the educator is selling a product and putting subtle pressure on colleagues to buy the product—colleagues feel that if they don't buy the product, the teacher will ignore them. The educator needs to go into the other job earlier than usual, and that requires that he leave his school position before the school day is over.

What about moonlighting as a tutor after school or in the summer? Many educators do this because of their teaching expertise, and certainly this provides a valuable service to many parents. At the same time, the educator should not utilize his position in order to solicit jobs as a tutor. If the educator puts an ad in the paper or advertises via word of mouth, he should not answer ads on work time. The educator should clarify with the school system what the policy is concerning tutoring students who are in the same school or who are in the same classroom. One can argue that the teacher who has had the student throughout the year knows the student the best and is in a good position to tutor that student, but again, the teacher cannot use his position to solicit those tutoring positions.

At times, school districts unintentionally create situations of conflicts of interest for teachers when they expect them to coach sports. The coaching of sports is a natural reality in the school, but for those educators who serve in both roles, they must be cognizant that the two roles should not impact negatively on each other. If they do, the individual must work with the school district personnel to resolve the differences. If differences cannot be resolved, then the teacher must make a decision about whether she can continue to coach.

Let's take the example of Marti. Marti is a fifth-grade teacher, and she is expected to coach the high school girls' volleyball team. She has learned quickly that coaching volleyball is taking up a great deal of her time during the day. There is a phone in her classroom, so parents of the girls are calling her and students are calling her. She is finding it difficult to teach because of these phone calls. Her dilemma is that she feels she should respond to the needs of her team. What should she do? A meeting with her principal assists her—the principal lets her know that during the school day her priority is to her fifth-grade students. Phone calls from players and their parents are restricted to her break times and to after-school hours when there are no meetings.

USE OF SCHOOL EQUIPMENT FOR PERSONAL USE

How many times have you walked into the teachers' lounge only to find an individual copying multiple recipes when you have classroom work to be copied? Someone is planning a party for the weekend and is copying invitations using the school's copy machine or laminating party decorations with the school's laminator. Schools should have policies about the appropriate use of school equipment for personal use; however, all teachers have the responsibility of monitoring their own behavior to make sure they are not abusing the system.

One might be able to justify a few copies of an item for personal use, but then there is the question of where to draw the line—how many copies is too many, is this copying taking time away from school work, is this copying really necessary? When in doubt, ask yourself these questions to help in your decision making.

The increase in computers in the schools has raised many new questions of ethics. All schools should have rules for the appropriate use of the computer, and many schools ask all users to sign an agreement that they will use the computer only for educational purposes related to their specific jobs. Educators must monitor their own behavior and set an example for their students. If while the students are working on independent work, they observe the teacher sitting at the computer playing solitaire, this sends a very bad message to students—that playing a game that is not related to instruction is acceptable in the school setting.

While educators are professionals, it remains very bothersome that there are still incidents being reported of teachers and administrators utilizing school computers to access pornographic sites. These individuals give a bad name to our profession.

USE OF SCHOOL TIME FOR PERSONAL RESPONSIBILITIES

Educators are given breaks during the school day, and those breaks can certainly be used to make doctor appointments, schedule children's carpools, or set up family events. However, spending time beyond breaks to engage in such activities may impact the education of the children with whom we are entrusted.

First and foremost in our minds when we are determining whether it is appropriate to use school time to make personal appointments is to ask ourselves the question "Am I taking away from the education of the children I have been given the responsibility to educate?" It is very difficult to juggle all of the responsibilities of having a family, growing professionally, and working full-time.

The reality of today's world is that as educators we may be taking care of not only our own children but also aging parents who may have significant needs. One of the authors remembers being very torn with trying to meet the needs of her aging mother while at the same time serving the children she was responsible for. She continually had to monitor that she was maintaining her work responsibilities.

Taking Classes for Advanced Degrees

A common dilemma faced by educators is the need to seek advanced degrees in order to move on the salary schedule or to advance professionally in the field. Some school districts or state departments of education require professional development to keep your position. Taking additional course work and engaging in professional development is critical in keeping current with the latest trends and gaining insights into your particular field. However, the authors have seen educators who make too many commitments, and then their educational position suffers. They then start doing course work during the school day when they are supposed to be working with children—this creates a conflict of interest. With more educators taking online classes, they may be doing class work online during the school day when they are supposed to be working with children.

Paperwork Responsibilities versus Direct Service to Children

Educators are faced with the very real problem of the overwhelming amount of paperwork that is required. This is particularly true for special educators who may have the responsibility of coordinating all of the IEPs for their students. Educators are torn—they need to collaborate with their peers, provide direct services to children, schedule meetings, work with parents, and do all of the paperwork. Couple these responsibilities with the responsibilities that educators have at home, and the educational system has created a major dilemma for educators. How do you get it all done without sacrificing direct services to children?

Let's use the example of Debra. Debra is a resource special education teacher who provides direct services to 25 students. She is supposed to assist classroom teachers with accommodations, provide direct services to children, and coordinate the IEPs of the students. She does not have the time to take her paperwork home because she has three young children there. She gets behind and has a deadline for getting three of her IEPs updated for IEP staffings that are coming up. She decides that she will give busy work to her students during third and fourth period so she can get her paperwork done. Has she compromised the education of her students? Has she found herself in a conflict of interest? She has not provided the services outlined on their IEPs; yet she is faced with paperwork deadlines. What could Debra do in this instance rather than compromising the education of her students?

Proactively she could take a couple of actions. When she works to develop her schedule, she can build time in for paperwork responsibilities, provided she meets the requirements of the time specified in each of the students' IEPs. She can also go to the principal and explain her needs and see whether there is some additional assistance that could be provided to her. Oftentimes, teachers are afraid to do this—they may fear that they should be Superman or Superwoman and should be able to do it all. They believe if they ask for help they are admitting a weakness. They may also believe that there is no way that the administrator will give them any assistance, but they don't know if they don't ask.

Debra does in fact go to the principal at her school, and he agrees to hire a substitute (a retired special educator) for her for a day so that she is able to get her IEPs done, and yet the students will still receive services because Debra is able to work closely with the substitute.

PLAYING FAVORITES WITH STAFF, STUDENTS, AND PARENTS

Positive or negative interactions with people can cause conflicts of interest. We may find ourselves in positions where we are not being fair to specific students, staff, or parents because of relationships with those individuals. Many school districts have specific rules about not hiring individuals who have a relative that works in the same building because of the awareness that such situations can cause conflicts of interest. Some teachers do not want to work in a school building where their own children go to school because they are afraid that conflicts of interest will arise. These are very difficult situations for educators. They know that they will treat differently (perhaps subconsciously) a niece or nephew who is in their class. Consistency and fairness are very difficult for any educator and become even more of a challenge when the educator is faced with a relative or a friend.

It is very difficult to be consistent and fair when the superintendent's son or the school board president's daughter is in your class or your best friend's son is on your debate team. All of these situations cause teachers to reflect continually on whether they are being fair to all of the children within the classroom.

The educator must recognize within himself that there could be a conflict of interest. It is a good idea for the educator to confer with the building administrator to determine whether another arrangement can be made. Your niece or nephew may be better served within another classroom, and frankly it may make your life a lot easier if you are not faced with the worry that something you say or do to your niece or nephew may cause family friction.

If this is not possible and you are faced with a student in your class who may potentially cause a conflict of interest, you must engage in continual reflection and monitor your own behavior to make sure you are being fair not only to that child but also to all of the students within your classroom.

Behavior problems in classrooms can be created when an educator treats a student differently than the other students. The teacher is often the antecedent for an inappropriate behavior from a student, and the teacher must make sure that she is not causing the particular problem. Keeping a log of a student's behavioral concerns may help the educator to see whether she is treating the student fairly.

In a previous book by these authors, *Surviving Internal Politics within the School* (2006), the topic of ostracism of fellow staff was discussed. Unfortunately, cliques can develop in schools where teachers are in the position of taking sides and playing favorites with their colleagues. While friendships are natural and are important to our well-being, ostracism is unhealthy and wreaks havoc with a school climate. We must always monitor our behavior to assure that because someone is not within our circle of friends we don't use that as an excuse to ostracize the individual. This creates a major conflict of interest—playing favorites with our friends and excluding others. The authors recommend that educators focus on kindness and set that example for our students. Students must see that we don't play favorites and are firm, fair, and consistent in our daily lives.

ACCEPTING MONIES FROM ANOTHER AGENCY THAT MIGHT CREATE A CONFLICT OF INTEREST

In schools, educators may write for grants from companies or agencies and receive a grant for implementing a particular program or for buying certain materials. The educator must be aware that with many of those grants there are "strings attached."

Before applying for a grant in the first place, the individual must read the fine print to determine what the specific expectations are for that grant. The individual may not be allowed to speak about a certain issue or may not be able to engage in specific types of activities as a result of receiving the grant. Educators may begin to feel as if the company or the agency owns them and they cannot engage in a number of activities that may have been important to them.

One of the authors was reminded of a teacher who was part of a schoolwide grant project. Money had been provided by a state agency. The state agency then required her, along with other staff members, to come to a state board meeting to report on the grant. The individuals were being expected to testify about how wonderful this grant project was and how the entire state should engage in this project. The teacher had testified, and a board member asked her a question about whether she had received any training to engage in the project. The answer the agency wanted her to give was that she had received training; but in reality she had not. She thought only for a second and told the truth—that, no, she had not received any training on how to implement this project. The author is sure that someone talked to her afterward to voice displeasure about her answer.

What if you have received a grant for a particular product—to buy a specific reading program or math or social studies program? You are enthused about using the program, and at first you think it is wonderful. As time moves on, you see that the children in your classroom are not keeping up with the program—it introduces new concepts too quickly. The children are not progressing, and now you fear that your test scores may reflect that lack of progress. You are afraid to be honest about the program because you fear that you will not receive any more materials, and your district has limited dollars to provide materials. In those dilemmas, remember that the responsibility that you have is to do what is best for your students, and you have the obligation to share your concerns.

Businesses may initiate projects in schools in order to promote their companies—such things as a specific banking program or a particular reward program for students. While these can be very beneficial for students, they can also give the impression that it is only that business that should be supported in the community. The educator has to weigh the pros and the cons of accepting those programs within the classroom.

The authors are, by no means, suggesting that school personnel should turn down assistance, but at the same time the educator must be careful that he or she is not promoting a particular product or service because of that program.

PERSONAL GAIN VERSUS PROFESSIONAL RESPONSIBILITY

Many people have ambitions to move into a better position. Certainly educators seek promotions or want a better classroom or want an increase in their classroom budgets. Such ambitions are admirable but should not be put ahead of the need to do what is right for the children within your classroom.

Picture this example of such a situation. Jennifer is currently a third-grade teacher and is doing an administrative internship with the principal within her school. The current principal is getting ready to retire next year, and Jennifer wants the job. A student within her classroom needs to be evaluated to determine whether there is a need for special education services. The mother of the student has asked for an evaluation. The principal does not want the evaluation conducted because the superintendent is pressuring him that the district has a referral rate that is too high. Jennifer has been involved in the Response to Intervention program within her school, and the student has received services through that program for over six months and is not progressing. Jennifer shows the data to the principal, but he says emphatically that the child will not be evaluated. Since Jennifer wants to be promoted within the district, she decides not to push the issue—let the next teacher deal with the problem.

Jennifer has put her need to advance in the school above the parent request and the needs of the child. She rationalizes that the student isn't going to lose that much time, but can she guarantee that the child will be able to catch up as a result of her failure to request the evaluation?

Here is another true-life example. George wants the job of the principal in his school building. He wants the current principal to leave so he can get the position. He begins to undermine the actions of the current principal and speaks negatively about the principal to his peers and to the school superintendent. He wants to push the principal out, and he has decided he will do whatever he needs to do to get the job.

At what cost will some individuals go to seek a promotion or personally gain favors? Unfortunately, there are individuals who will do whatever it takes to get ahead. They have indeed lost sight of ethical behavior. They have begun to rationalize that their actions are permissible to get ahead. Will their actions "catch up with them"? In many cases they will. The superintendent of George's school district is very ethical and does not approve of what George has done in order to get the job. The superintendent therefore will not give George the job as principal and in fact will not write him a letter of recommendation to go to another school district. Other teachers in the building saw what George was really like and are very disappointed in his behavior. They become very cautious in their work with George.

The bottom line is that at the end of the day you must be able to look yourself in the mirror and know that you have done the right thing, even though it may have cost you a promotion. The promotion is not worth it when someone engages in unethical behavior.

Making Your Resume Look Good for Personal Gain

A recent situation occurred in the life of one of the authors. An individual wanted to get ahead in her particular work environment. She therefore accepted a responsibility in a volunteer organization so she could put it on her resume. When she accepted the responsibility, she knew she had no intentions of engaging in any of the work involved; she just wanted to "pad" her resume. Was that ethical behavior? No. She knew that she was not going to do any of the work that was expected, but she was excited about the thought that she could make her resume look impressive and could also get her way paid to meetings in a large city.

Another practice that some educators engage in is to prepare a proposal for a state or national conference. They want to be able to put the presentation on their resume. They get accepted for the program and then don't show up for the conference. Some never had any intention of going to the particular conference. The information, however, is still on their resume. They fail to mention they did not attend.

Educators must be very cautious to depict reality on their resume. Only truthful activities and events should be on the resume. We may all remember that some individuals earned an advanced degree from a "mail-order" university. They put the degree on their resume and failed to disclose from where the degree was received. They used the degree to seek advancement on the district's salary schedule. When the district determined where the degrees were from, they did not honor the degrees, and it also left a "black mark" on the records of those individuals.

Educators must be as specific as possible about their work history, their honors, their publications, and so on.

DISCLOSING POTENTIAL CONFLICTS OF INTEREST

There will be times when any educator is going to have a conflict of interest. The educator is the president of the local teachers' union and will need to separate out that role from the role of the classroom teacher. The educator is receiving a grant that, in fact, clouds that individual's thoughts about a particular program. The educator has his niece in the classroom. So many times, the educator is wearing two hats—one of those hats impacts his viewpoint and behavior about the other hat. When the educator is in such a position, he must have the honesty to disclose that information.

A teacher may serve as a school board member in one district and teach in another. A situation arises where the two districts are to engage in a special project, and a vote is required—the educator must disclose that there is a conflict of interest and must excuse herself from the vote. We often hear people say, "I am wearing my _____ hat and see the situation from that perspective." It is much better to be safe and disclose the information than to allow a conflict to cloud your decision making.

Educators must be very careful that they are not engaging in unethical behavior through the process of omission. They are not sure what they should disclose, so they just say nothing and hope that the information will not be disclosed.

Let's take the example of the classroom teacher who is preparing for an IEP meeting. Right before the IEP meeting, the teacher receives a report from a physician, and that physician's report does not support what the teacher is planning to recommend. The teacher decides to just file the report and not share the information with the IEP team. Clearly, the teacher engaged in behavior that is not ethical—he withheld necessary information.

In order to be honest about a potential conflict of interest, the educator must recognize that potential himself. Oftentimes educators may fool themselves by self-talk, saying to themselves that they will remain neutral and they won't allow their conflict to cloud their judgment. However, we are all humans and sometimes cannot see the impact of some of our actions. We must look carefully at ourselves to determine whether we are being objective in our actions. When in doubt, speak with your immediate supervisor to determine whether there may be a conflict, and continually evaluate your own behavior to determine whether you are acting in an ethical manner. When in doubt, it is wise to abstain from a vote that could be construed as a conflict of interest.

SUMMARY

Every day in our schools, we as educators are responsible for being positive role models for our students, and we must remember that every action we take impacts our students. Each of us also represents the entire educational community, and all we do represents our profession within the community and within the greater society. We must monitor any conflicts of interest that arise within our work. We must live up to the highest standards of ethical behavior and must therefore monitor our own behavior closely to assure that we are excellent molders of future generations and are positive ambassadors of the educational profession.

REFERENCE

Johns, B., McGrath, M., and Mathur, S. 2006. *Surviving internal politics within the school*. Lanham, MD: Rowman & Littlefield Education.

CHAPTER 5

The Cost of Borderline Actions

Carl was hired as a principal of a charter school. This charter school had experienced staff and faculty turnover during the past couple of years. When Carl received the contract, Jason, the superintendent of the Mayflower School District, advised Carl that he should start thinking about making changes in the personnel. What he meant was that Carl may have to come up with a plan for getting rid of some people. According to the superintendent, there were people on the staff and faculty who were not performing well. He also added that the previous principal was not a good personnel manager, and he lacked leadership skills. He was unable to make some tough decisions.

Carl had a master's degree in leadership and business management. Prior to seeking this job, he had worked in a residential setting and managed a day support program for students who had mental health issues. On his first day on the job, he started planning how to approach the personnel issues that were shared with him. He knew he couldn't just act on assumptions and start firing people. He needed to know how faculty really worked. He began to pay attention to the working habits of staff and faculty.

Carl quickly found out students were not participating in any extracurricular activities because teachers did not stay for after-school activities. He called a meeting and emphasized the importance of extracurricular activities that supplemented the regular school curriculum and supported the needs and interests of students. A few examples that he shared were honor societies, publications, athletic teams, and other extensions of classroom work. The purpose of these activities was to promote character-building qualities of participation and leader-ship. He further explained how a fund-raiser could secure money for student activities or equipment and how it could provide a great way for getting to know parents. He found that many faculty members did not say much during the meeting, but as soon as they went back to their lounge they started bickering about the new ideas.

After a week or so, Carl started asking faculty members individually if they were willing to learn more about extracurricular programs and would like to get involved in them. First, he found there was a lack of interest among the members, and they did not want to participate in that. But then Susan asked a question: "What would I have to do if I were to be involved in a fund-raiser?" He told her that first they needed to find out what would be a good fund-raiser for this school (e.g., sell-ing baked goods or magazines) as well as determine safety and health needs. Then, they needed to involve paraprofessionals, parents, and other staff members in this fund-raiser. He encouraged her to talk to other faculty members to find out their ideas.

A week later, Susan and Pat began to plan the event. In the meantime, the superintendent really wanted Carl to start documenting the prob-lems with his staff. After about a month or so, he asked how Carl liked his job. Carl went to Jason's office and told him how great his experi-ence working with Pat and Susan was.

Jason gave him a little spiel about the last principal, Bob, and reit-erated that the last principal was ineffective in dealing with the faculty. Jason added that the last principal left because faculty, like Susan and Pat, were not paying attention to what needed to be done and gave him a hard time. Carl shared with him that he was noticing some growth in faculty members. He told him that it would take a while for faculty to understand his new ideas and suggestions. But in general he found them quite supportive of his new ideas. Jason was surprised at Carl's positive attitude.

Carl could not stop noticing that Pat was always coming late to school. He asked her to make an appointment to talk to him. Should he follow the advice that he was receiving from his superior, Jason, and go ahead on the plan of documenting Pat's late arrivals? Or, should he pay attention to what was going on in Pat's life? Without sounding too preachy or controversial, he wanted to raise his awareness about *larger questions and challenges that were associated within the school. He decided to ignore for a while that Pat was coming late to school. The issues of parent involvement and additional funding to support arts and music were more important for him. He really wanted to make the best charter school in the valley. He was unsure how he could achieve his goal without faculty support. Because of his social skills and leadership style, faculty members were doing better than they had with the previous principal.*

There are times that we all go through such dilemmas where we want to produce quick results, but we forget that we are dealing with people. Carl thought maybe he should share his apprehension, uncertainty, concerns, goals, and commitments with his faculty members. When Carl met with Pat he realized that she had a real issue. He found that she was a single mother, and she had to leave her child at preschool before she came to teach. The preschool was in the opposite direction. It took at least 45 minutes to get to the preschool from her house and then an additional 30 minutes to come to work. He found out about some good preschools closer to the charter school where Pat worked and asked her if she was interested in sending her child to the surrounding preschools. Pat found Carl to be very supportive, caring, and empathetic, which was very different from what she had seen in Bob, the principal before Carl. Bob was detached and had no desire to know about other people's lives.

Carl figured out that it was not just the faculty and staff that had issues; his predecessor, Bob, had issues too, and his limited leadership skills contributed to problems. He did not provide sufficient direction. He was never there to discuss faculty issues. He spent most of his time attending meetings at the district office.

Carl, on the other hand, was willing to find out how things could work with faculty and staff. He wanted to support them and provide resources to them to be successful. Carl did not feel it was right for him to follow his superintendent's advice and take drastic steps of firing people. He believed in ethical decision making.

Ethical decision making is making decisions that empower people to produce better results. The purpose is not to diminish or undermine other people's professional goals or create more personal problems for them, but to make them aware of the impact of their actions. If Pat comes late, how does her consistent late arrival negatively affect children, faculty, and parents? It is important for Carl to make sound decisions, decisions that are going to produce long-term positive effects. If he lets Pat do whatever she wants to, the superintendent is going to be on his case.

A month later, Jason asked Carl to identify people who should not receive their contracts for the following year. Clearly, Jason was using a business model to show that he was an efficient leader; he did not want to support faculty who were not performing to his standards. On the other hand, Carl believed in professional growth and learning; he knew his staff and faculty had the capacity to improve and refine their skills. This case provides an example of ethical dilemmas challenging our professional practice.

This chapter describes situations that educators usually deal with, situations that warrant emergency decision making or may need quick fixes. In the decision-making process, "borderline ethical" practices are characterized as ways that are necessary to survive but may have long-term subtle effects that produce negative outcomes. We make decisions on a daily basis and choose right from wrong. It is important to see that we do not always compromise the integrity of the decision-making process.

BORDERLINE ETHICS

The term *borderline ethics* is used in the business world, where success is defined by making profit and monetary gains. Businesses may decide on reducing the cost of their products, not just to make up the sale but to intentionally weaken the competition. A construction company may hire employees, giving them a significantly low salary or hiring them part-time without providing them compensatory benefits, just to increase profitability.

What are the implications when these borderline practices are adopted in education? No one profits when students do not receive education. Students who drop out have erratic employment, mental health problems, and poor quality of life. Despite this existing knowledge and professional wisdom about negative outcomes associated with dropping out, many students are deprived of an appropriate education. What prevents these students from receiving an education? How much of it can be attributed to poor decision making on the part of the school systems? Apparently, somewhere along the way, some people could not make sound decisions or perhaps engaged in borderline ethical practices that prevented these students from receiving services.

Here is another example of borderline ethics. Susan was a special education teacher who attended an IEP meeting at 2:30 on Monday. Michael, an eight-year-old student identified as having emotional and behavioral problems, was known to engage in disruptive behavior and lacked self-regulation. The general education teacher, Natasha, had tried a couple of prereferral strategies that included teaching self-monitoring skills for about a month. As we all know, research and professional knowledge emphasize that these techniques should be taught for a longer period of time to show effects; however, Natasha's eagerness in this IEP meeting became apparent because she wanted Michael to be placed in a special education setting.

On the contrary, Susan thought that Michael could benefit from a regular education setting with some supports, if the teacher was willing to make some adjustments. Michael's parents, the general education teacher, the social worker, and the school psychologist came to the meeting in order to discuss Michael's case. The discussion focused on Michael's inappropriate behaviors. Susan said that she was willing to take Michael out for about an hour and would teach self-control and other social skills necessary for him to function effectively. Natasha was not ready for that option and convinced the parents and the psychologist that Michael would not at all benefit in her classroom and needed to be placed in a special education classroom.

The school psychologist suggested that since there was no emotional and behavioral disorders (EBD) classroom in this school, Michael would be placed in a classroom with children with mild to moderate mental retardation. Susan reminded the psychologist that the evaluation indicated regulation and hyperactivity issues leading to the diagnosis of emotional disabilities. The psychologist pointed out that the label did not matter and that Michael was likely to benefit from this placement.

Susan felt that she was pushed away from serving Michael, who clearly had emotional issues. Without appropriate educational services, and social interventions, she knew that children with EBD are at a significant risk for school failure and mental health and adjustment problems. As a result, they are more likely to drop out of school, stay unemployed, engage in delinquent behavior, and have unsuccessful interpersonal relationships. However, she did not want to create a power struggle between herself and the psychologist.

Cognizant of the shortfalls of this decision, she engaged in the behavior of compliance and did not lead the path of finding the right choice for this student. She began to question herself and thought she needed to be flexible in her thinking; she was unaware of the risks of flexibility and adaptability. She could have asked for more information in this meeting if she was feeling unsure. How could she prevent herself from getting pressured in this situation and remain objective? How could she keep herself away from being confused and not contribute to a bad decision?

It is important to be deliberate in decision making and reflect upon the long-term, broad impact of your decisions. The most difficult situations arise when faced with strong pressure to take an action that is "borderline" ethical or when two ethical standards conflict.

WHEN DO PEOPLE OPT FOR BORDERLINE ETHICAL PRACTICES?

Contradictory Information

When teachers are unsure about issues or receive contradictory information, they fail to develop a true sense of what is relevant and meaningful for the student. It is important that educators rely on expert advice, professional wisdom, and research. The need for careful examination of information is extremely important. When we hear phrases like "all students can learn" or "inclusion for all" and we don't even know what these statements actually mean, we need to become more objective in our thinking.

Susan was consistently receiving contradictory information from Natasha, the general education teacher, and the psychologist. She probably thought it was better to capitulate when no one else seemed to be agreeing with what she had to say, even though inside her heart she knew she was right.

Different Views about the Same Issue

When people receive different points of view, they tend to pick the one that appears to be most amicable with their thinking. When new ideas seem to fit in with their own views, they find inquiry aimless and ineffective. For example, there are different views on how children with EBD should be taught. Should they be taught by specialists or generalists? Should they be taught by a teacher who is emergency certified or special education certified in EBD? Should the teachers of students with EBD go through the teacher preparation program that lasts longer or the one that has a fast track? Do programs that are too short in duration offer the same quality of experience as compared to the ones that are longer? All these questions have two sides. It depends on the source of our information. We may receive a different answer from a researcher who inquires about such questions or a practitioner who relies on conventional wisdom. Clearly, we need to explore all the possible information before we make a decision. We know that professionals represent various perspectives or conceptualizations, and children need a varied and comprehensive approach to dealing with their academic and behavioral issues. Despite varied points of inquiry, it is important that we provide consistent directions to teachers and empower them enough when they make ethical decisions.

Overemphasis on Compliance

In recent years, we have noticed tremendous pressure put on teachers to comply with state and federal standards. It is not bad to have standards, but it is important that compliance to these standards be naturally satisfying for teachers. They do not comply merely because of external pressures that, in their views, have no value or meaning. If compliance results in better outcomes for students, they are likely to feel positive.

Flexibility and Adaptability

Oftentimes when teachers are involved in a collaborative decision-making process, they are encouraged to develop listening skills and flexibility in their thinking. Such team processes require educators to engage in a systematic process of identifying problems, generating solutions, and evaluating solutions. While knowing what the right thing is, they do not take a firm stance on doing the right thing because they want to show their good listening skills and want to hear other people's views. In the earlier example, where Susan had to participate in the IEP meeting for Michael, she knew that the best possible placement for him was a regular education setting with some resource supports, but the team members pushed for a self-contained mental retardation (MR) classroom for him. Susan could not convince the team members of why she was thinking that way. Even today, she feels guilty for not speaking her mind and asserting her views.

Oftentimes It Is an Unintentional Process

Most educators do not intentionally engage in borderline ethical practices. Oftentimes, they seem to have limited information to make a decision that is in favor of the student. For example, studies suggest that prereferral interventions prevent false positives where students without special needs get referred for special education services when they do not need these services. But we find that general educators do not necessarily employ prereferral interventions as often as they should. Not only that, they often find themselves not well versed in dealing with a wide array of social and behavioral issues. Sometimes they don't understand how their limited knowledge and lack of interest in special needs have a functional relationship with applicable ethical standards and affect outcomes for students with disabilities.

SUBTLE PRESSURES FROM ADMINISTRATORS

Teachers sometimes do not know how to deal with pressures from authority figures, supervisors, parents, and administrators. They do not know how to handle subtle pressures from administrators who are less interested in the performance of individual students with EBD and more concerned with an overarching goal of making adequate yearly progress (AYP). They do not know how to deal with difficult parents who seem to disagree with whatever the teacher believes in. A good-faith referral is one that is driven solely by the best interests of the student, in this case the student with EBD. Referring a student to special education because of a desire to raise accountability ratings would not be considered a good-faith referral. On the other hand, failing to provide services to a student with EBD who needs these services is unethical. But we hear about cases where the principal subtly pressured the IEP team in a certain direction to make certain types of decisions that were not necessarily in favor of the student.

One may wonder what might be some of the motivation for the principal to do this. We have also heard of cases where administrators were punitive toward special education teachers when they advocated for a child with special needs. For instance, a principal may have an issue of funding and finds himself incapable of adhering to the special education recommendations.

CONFLICTING PRESSURES FROM POLICIES

Policies are supposed to provide guidance for better services for children. In an article on zero tolerance, Russ Skiba and Reece Peterson (1999) define zero tolerance as "policies that punish all offenses severely, no matter how minor," and they clearly indicate long-term negative effects of such policies. One of the results of these policies is that a high percentage of students who show problem behaviors are currently served in exclusionary or alternative settings.

Exclusionary settings are supposedly the last resort for some serious cases, but administrators and general educators use these settings immediately to get some students out of school. They seem to forget about the fact that these students have a right—a right to an appropriate education and a least restrictive environment. The intent of IDEA was to ensure that every student with special needs was provided with a free and appropriate education. Despite the passage of this law, it is still difficult for some professionals to provide appropriate services to children of certain exceptionalities such as EBD. It is hard to imagine how things would have turned out if we didn't have these policies in place. The intent of IDEA was always to produce better outcomes for students with special needs.

On the other hand, with the passage of the No Child Left Behind Act in 2001, the focus was shifted to all children. The law emphasized accountability for student achievement for *all* students and resulted in increased attention on how to or whether to apply high-stakes assessment to students with special needs. This high-stakes accountability created conflict between general educators, administrators, and special educators. Professionals began to question the appropriateness of holding students with special needs accountable to the same academic content standards as their normative peers. The ethical dilemma is whether these students should be viewed within the concept of *all* students or should be excluded from the accountability standards for some specific reasons. As mentioned in chapter 2, sometimes educators unintentionally justify exclusion without thinking that someone is feeling excluded. Or, they may be demanding inclusion simply on the basis of principle when it is not in the best interest of an individual student.

COMPETING LOYALTIES

Oftentimes, educators find they are facing conflict in loyalties. For example, should they be listening to parents of students with EBD and provide services to them in inclusionary settings? Or should they be attending to the principal and put them in a self-contained setting without least restrictive provisions? Should they be teaching social skills to these students, or should they be worrying about their academics? Should they be guiding their instruction based upon what they know from research, or should they be listening to the principal of the school, who does not care about research and finds it meaningless?

Educators need to develop the ability to apply ethical principles effectively in clinical decision making; they should be able to foresee how ethical decision-making processes function within the context of service delivery. They should know about the "side effects" of punishment or other procedures; and they should also not forget about the rights to treatment of students with EBD or other disabilities and their families. They should make themselves aware of conflicts that are created by the laws of education. For example, with the passage of NCLB, are we truly arguing for success for *all*, and if so, why do we allow suspension and expulsion to exclude *some* students from coming to school? How can we leave no child behind when some students with special needs cannot attend school? They should be concerned about these questions and should not show allegiance to only one side of the problem; they need to look at the whole picture.

By implementing a districtwide discipline policy of expulsion in an inner-city school, where students are asked to remain out of school until their parents can come to school to meet with school officials, are we truly meeting the purpose of discipline? This policy may be well intentioned, but it is important to ask what it enforces and who is best served in this decision: the school or the student?

ETHICAL ISSUES OF RESEARCH

We rely on research for evidence. Whatever research states, we believe that it has some element of truth. But we also know that oftentimes research findings using a large sample size do not necessarily show ways of categorization that obscure within-group or individual differences. Oftentimes, findings from research are not clearly reflecting the changes in the intervention associated with changes in the outcomes. For example, research indicates that students with behavior problems engage in disruptive behaviors, but it does not show how disruptive behavior is also related to the level of system supports. Research also indicates that students with EBD in the self-contained classrooms have more internalizing behaviors as compared to those in the self-contained school. So what does this mean? Every contradictory finding calls on researchers for additional explanation. Most importantly, these findings emphasize that we need to be fully aware of ethical responsibilities regarding the design, formal approval, implementation, and evaluation of data-based research and its implications.

HOW DO YOU MAKE ETHICAL DECISIONS?

Develop Ethical Mindfulness

Ethical mindfulness refers to a process aimed at decreasing uncertainty and developing strategies for better professional conduct (Francis, 2002). Politicians and businesspeople engage in the tactics of creating ambiguity about issues to promote themselves or their products.

In education, we need to have clarity in thinking because we are in the profession of providing services to children. It also means we need to understand the difference between solving and resolving a situation.

"Solving a problem" means looking at a better long-term outcome, whereas "resolving" is merely fixing an immediate problem and having to continue to fix it for a long time. Ethical mindfulness is separate from ethical codes of behavior. Francis (1999) provides further guidance for ethical practice and draws our attention to how it differs from following ethical rules and codes. The first condition is that educators engage in practices that are effective. Effective practices are those that create long-term effects and benefits for students and not just focus upon changing short-term quick fixes.

The second condition is that professionals be able to distinguish between intentions and results of a practice. In other words, they keep the intentions in mind before they get too involved in producing results. Remember, good intentions sometimes may not produce good results immediately and may take a while in producing good results.

The third condition is that professionals combine rational reasoning with humanistic values and intuitive insights when processing information and arriving at conclusions. They must be aware of the limitations of ethical codes that are based only on external ordinances such as Department of Education regulations or school policies, which are not derived from good intent and internal qualities such as honesty, generosity, and compassion (Francis, 1999; Francis, 2002).

Are leaders who have the burden of decision making aware of these conditions? Research on ethics, some of which stretches back 36 years, suggests school superintendents confronted with ethical dilemmas can be expected to make decisions consistent with the AASA Code of Ethics less than 50 percent of the time. The findings raise concerns about leadership preparation.

Engage in Database Decision Making

Better decision making relies on appropriate and ethical use of data. It implies that a school has taken the necessary precautions and steps to ensure that data are accurate, valid, and reliable and that the analytical process is complete, equitable, and fair. If schools follow a continuous improvement process for planning and decision making, the results will be easily linked back to specific questions, goals, and problems.

We also acknowledge that data do not magically appear to provide evidence of success and solve all of the school's problems. We have to learn where to get data, how to manage data, how to ask good questions about the data, how to analyze the data accurately, and how to apply data results. Sometimes deliberate or accidental abuse of data is likely in this process, and the application of knowledge must always be subordinate to morality.

We need to engage in systematic evaluation and review of institutional purposes, practices, roles, responsibilities, and outcomes and provide ourselves a period of introspection and reflection by avoiding the "bandwagon" mentality. We need to pay attention to our personal beliefs as educators by steering clear of a superficial desire to be on a winning side all the times.

Identify Soft Signs of Unethical Behaviors

Ethical mindfulness is not something that appears all of a sudden. It needs to be taught. Professionals require training to develop this skill. If ethical practices are not encouraged or reinforced in a system, one can begin to see the soft signs of ethical collapse (Jennings, 2006). In this first sign of ethical collapse, there is not just a reasonable focus on numbers and results but often an unreasonable and unrealistic *obsession* with meeting quantitative goals.

How can we prevent this from happening? Jennings (2006) suggests surrounding the goal achievements in a square box of values so that we are not looking at results without ethical processes. In this framework, we can now consider new and more desirable ways to deal with the issue of testing the relatively small group of students who don't seem to fit into the alternate assessments states have designed under IDEA or the general state assessments required for most students.

SUMMARY

So what is missing from this profession? We need better decision makers. We need to be one of them. We'll become sure that we are doing the right things for students as we make sound decisions at every step. Always remember your work goes beyond you; your decisions today will affect tomorrow. Emergency decision making affects long-term outcomes. Please do not forget to continue to ask relevant questions, and remember your commitment to children and families and their educational pursuits. You may feel the pressure from external forces, but remember to always keep in mind the end goal—educating students and doing the right thing for them.

REFERENCES

Francis, R. 1999. Background to Ethics. In *Ethics for psychologists: A handbook*. Leicester: British Psychological Society.

Francis, R. 2002. The need for a professional ethic: International perspectives. *Educational and Child Psychology* 19(1): 7–15.

Jennings, M. M. 2006. *The seven signs of ethical collapse: Understanding what causes moral meltdowns in organizations*. New York: St. Martin's Press.

Skiba, R., & Peterson, R. 1999. The dark side of zero tolerance: Can punishment lead to safe schools? *Phi Delta Kappan* 80(5): 372–76, 381–82.

CHAPTER 6

Difficulties Faced in "Doing the Right Thing"

Corita began a teaching job in a new city. She felt happy to start over after a bitter divorce. Bringing her daughter, Tina, with her was a delight. She felt relief after months of legal entanglement. At last, with her dignity intact, she could move forward and make a fresh start. She arranged to see a therapist weekly and found a church near her new condo. Corita also decided to use the church day-care center to keep Tina's relationships more consistent. Things were heading to a new normal. Life was looking up.

When Corita arrived at her new job as a secondary Spanish teacher, she found excellent working conditions, including adequate supplies, books, and resources. She hoped that this would be a year in which she would be able to regain ground, not only personally but professionally as well.

After a few weeks Corita gradually got acquainted with the staff on her hall. She enjoyed her students and believed things were beginning to roll along at a steady pace from day to day. Corita often ate lunch late, as she preferred to take her prep during the noon hour when the lounge was busy. Having a quiet meal with fewer teachers seemed to work out well for her. When it seemed she would have more work to take home, Corita corrected papers while she ate so she would have more free time in the evening to spend with her daughter.

During one of her lunch periods, another teacher invited Corita to consider a pyramid business opportunity. If she would sell health products under the supervision of Danielle, the French teacher, she could earn extra money. Danielle, having heard Corita mention her divorce, thought Corita a perfect prospect for expanding her home-based business.

Feigning interest in Corita's daughter and circumstances over several weeks, Danielle formulated a sales plan to enlist Corita into her company. In fact, Danielle brought samples and products to school and left them on Corita's desk, even while Corita was engaged in teaching a lesson on verbs. Danielle's actions to recruit Corita increased in frequency as she aimed to add her to her business grouping.

Corita enjoyed Danielle and wanted to develop a friendship. When Danielle invited her to an after-school product display set up by special e-mail invitation, Corita thought it would be fun to sample the products and enjoy some conversation with Danielle and her exclusive group of teachers.

Corita interpreted Danielle's request that she not tell others about this gathering as an affirmation that she was "in" with Danielle's group. Danielle's intention, however, was to protect herself from being found out, as she was doing business on school time and using her classroom computer to invite staff to the party. School policy forbade such activities.

After the low-profile party, Corita received a form to fill out that would make her an official salesperson working under Danielle in the pyramid. If Corita sold a certain amount of products, both she and Danielle would make extra money. Danielle suggested that this business relationship would give them more time to enjoy one another's company and catch up on school news.

Each day when Corita stopped to pick up her daughter at day care, she met another single mom, Anna, who also attended her church. Anna invited her to a single-parent supper complete with child care at the community center. Anna asked if she could bring Tina and come on the spur of the moment. Considering that she had no plans for the evening, Corita agreed.

The two young women took their children to the child-care room, where they would enjoy a meal of macaroni and cheese and other kid foods while the adults ate a catered meal from the local deli. Corita breathed a sigh of relief at the opportunity to actually visit with someone in her situation and not have to cook as well.

The two women sat down and met other single parents. As their conversations progressed, one of them, Pete, brought up the fact that a man at his job site was let go for using company time and resources to build *his side brokerage business. He not only used the computers and tele-phones to make contacts but also worked a deal with his secretary to answer the phone in a general way so callers could not tell if they were reaching his place of business or his "brokerage firm."*

This guy supplied his secretary with her favorite candy and soda on a regular basis, and she willingly answered the phone with the neutral script that he had supplied for her. Ultimately, Pete and others in the office figured out what was happening. When word reached the CEO, this man's minutes at the business were numbered. His next step was to set up the "brokerage firm" in his apartment and answer his own calls.

As Corita listened to this story, she rooted for the CEO and ac-claimed those in the office who stood up to this man for going against office policy. Then the day-care attendant made an announcement that the children were about to join the parents for a dessert of fresh, warm apple pies with cinnamon ice cream. When the event ended, Corita and Anna left feeling pleased that they had attended this meal.

That night after Corita tucked Tina into bed, she sat in her easy chair to relax and review her day. Though she had had a delightful day both at Danielle's special gathering and at the supper for single parents, something nagged her. It had been such a busy day; perhaps she should go to bed and get some rest. After all, tomorrow she would be on deck again with her students.

The following morning, Corita began her lesson in a creative man-ner. Her students paid special attention as they dialogued in simple Spanish sentences. Right in the middle of her lesson, Danielle came in and using a demanding tone asked her for the business form. She had expected it returned and signed before classes began. Danielle acted as if she were in another realm, not in a school.

Corita's students heard their conversation and even the name of Danielle's business. Corita tried to tell Danielle that she would talk to her at lunchtime. After many suggestions from Corita that she needed to continue the lesson, Danielle finally left the room. Though Corita tried hard, she couldn't recapture the connection she had with her stu-dents previous to Danielle's interruption.

When Corita entered the staff lounge, Danielle again spoke impa-tiently to her and even described the ultimate possibility of earning a va-cation to a resort if she was able to make a certain sales quota. Being busy, Corita had not until this moment processed the nagging feeling she had had the night before. Danielle's side business run from school was similar to the one Pete described at the supper the night before. She had just been too busy to make the connection.

Corita knew she wanted no part of Danielle's health product company, her group, or her scheming. Corita also knew that she had an ethical decision to make. She wondered if Pete would meet her for coffee and some coaching on how to handle this situation. She was not going to buckle to Danielle's pressure and get involved with this sales "opportunity."

FACING UNETHICAL PRESSURES

All workplaces present individuals with both opportunities and pressures. Often educators such as Corita find themselves pressured to go off track and get involved in other activities unrelated to the job. Sometimes those in power in a workplace set up circumstances whereby workers have to choose between acceptance and ethical treatment of others at their school or in their district.

In the film *Freedom Writers*, Hilary Swank played a beginning teacher known as Mrs. G., assigned to a newly integrated high school in Los Angeles. She began her job with the desire to help students from disadvantaged backgrounds learn to love literature. Her department head, Miss Campbell, suggested she use simplified, condensed versions of literature books. In addition she inferred that her job would be babysitting. Low expectations from school leadership immediately put Mrs. G. into an ethical challenge.

As the story progressed, Mrs. G. found ways to reach her challenging and challenged students. Students read *Romeo and Juliet* and *The Diary of Anne Frank* and saw themes in these stories that they could apply to their own lives.

Mrs. G. received pressure from the school site-based management team to follow practices that had been typical at the school. They did not approve of her way of teaching. In order to remain true to herself and give her students the experiences she believed they needed, she chose to go over the heads of building leadership and seek support at the district office.

When the school year drew to a close, Mrs. G. realized that her students had developed a sense of family and safety in her classroom. Her students wanted to stay together, keeping her as their teacher for a second year, but this was against school practice. She sought support from district administration, as her school administration refused her request to keep the group for another school year.

The decision did not come without challenge from Miss Campbell, who went for Mrs. G.'s vulnerable spot. The department head pointed out that Mrs. G. was currently going through a divorce and thus accused her of wanting to keep this class in order to have a sense of family for herself.

Seeing Mrs. G as a teacher of integrity and honesty who expressed clearly and consistently what she wanted for her students, top administration overruled the school leaders and granted Mrs. G. the opportunity to continue to build on the successes students experienced in her English class. This film illustrated that pressure tactics motivated by professional jealousy did not win out over sincere efforts to better the educational and social conditions of students.

As *Freedom Writers* illustrated, pressure brought out the best in the character of a teacher. When asked to do less or to do what is wrong, the true character of an individual comes to the surface. In his recent book *The Shame of the Nation* (2005), Jonathan Kozol tells of a teacher working in the inner city who told him of an instance where she had been pressured to go along with pretense. She had observed papers posted in the hall with student work erased and rewritten by the teachers themselves.

The principal believed that students would be proud to see their work displayed. The teacher, on the contrary, believed that students would not feel good about seeing their work erased and replaced by teacher writing. When this teacher told the principal that she would not doctor student work and put it on display, she was warned that a communication would be placed in her file. Kozol reports that another teacher received a warning about getting such a letter in his file for the same reason (pp. 81–82).

Kozol also reports a heroic action of another educator who took a stand on ethical values. Seattle teachers told him about David Engle, Ballard High School principal, who resigned on principle. When Engle heard of a federal court decision removing the factor of race known as the "tiebreaker" in admissions policy, he saw it as a move against integration. Engle wanted to model an ethical response to students in his school who valued the diversity of their high school (p. 218).

Some educators face pressures of great magnitude whereby they have to determine if they will go along with the crowd and with the system or if they need to take a stand. Often the character of these teachers or principals will not allow them to simply stand back or sit silently while unethical events, both major or even small, occur. All matter.

SMALL BUT CHALLENGING PRESSURES

Some pressures come in the form of daily challenges. For instance, if a teacher who has been depriving students of their just due educationally comes to the union for defense, what does a local organization do in response? How can union officers defend someone who was slacking off on fulfilling students' IEPs? Perhaps instead of trying to defend the indefensible they could contribute to the greater good by assisting the teacher to improve teaching methods through a mentor or time management coach.

They could also diplomatically work to bridge the gap between school and home to, in a sense, make amends for the teacher's educational errors. Wise union officers know how to create a win-win situation out of difficulties.

Teachers who do not "carry their weight" not only impact the progress of students but also deter teams from fulfilling their full responsibilities. Some teams choose to go without a teacher who fails to give just due to the goals of the group. Others decide to bring the teacher on board through affirmation, invitation, and even confrontation.

When a team is unsuccessful in efforts to gain the full effort of a team member, an administrator, department head, or neutral party for the union, staff development department, or counseling department may be needed. Such persons have the skills to help connect the unconnected and unite fragmented staff groupings.

Not all such situations mend easily. One of the authors learned of a situation whereby a teacher offered less to her team than was expected. However, since this teacher was a personal friend of the principal's, the team felt that their hands were tied when they wanted the principal's assistance in addressing the situation. Creative teams, however, come up with solutions for potentially unsolvable situations when they remain determined and open to possibilities.

Temptation comes in various forms to teachers, as it does to everyone. When the school year becomes difficult, tempers grow shorter, and some students test the nerves of the best professionals. When this combination converges, the option of cutting corners comes into play. For example, suppose Mrs. Anderson finds a flyer in the mailbox announcing an all-day science experience for students who show potential to study further and go on in the field.

Mrs. Anderson imagines a day without three students. Though they show her no potential or interest in science, the absence of these children with learning and behavior problems offers her a day without difficulty. It is spring, and a classroom without Joey, Jeff, and Jenny sounds like a ticket to sanity. Will Mrs. Anderson slip their names onto the registration list? Sounds timely and tempting, but is such an action ethical?

Time is often of the essence in schools. As with Mrs. Anderson, teachers face pressure to get involved in conversations that detract from lesson planning and take them from focus on their professional priorities.

For a minute, maybe Mabel would like to help us get the shower guest list ready on district time. Would Paul plan his weekend and pay his bills while supervising study hall? Might Marilyn make a few calls to her mother and sister once she started her students on an art project? Certainly Cheryl can slip in a second before students arrive to order a novel online.

One of the authors overheard a conversation between a receptionist and a solicitor. This receptionist modeled ethical boundaries between her duties and the option of distraction provided by the unwelcome solicitor.

After attempts to discourage the caller, the receptionist, with patience and assertiveness, finally told the determined salesperson something like the following: "This is a business. I have work to do right now that I am being paid to handle. I am not paid to have this conversation. Thank you for your time. I am going to hang up on you. I need to hang up now." (Click.)

This vignette illustrates to educators that there are limits on valuable school time. Often temptations and lures from personal interests and responsibilities as well as the agendas of others offer distractions from duties. As the business pays the receptionist to ward off distraction and make her time count, so does a school district expect that time on the job be given in the best interest of students, staff, and families.

BEING ABOUT THE BUSINESS OF EDUCATION

Practices from the business world benefit education in examples such as the one just given. But does the influence of business models always bring about the best in the educational culture? For example, let's say that Joe, Julie, and Janet have taught middle school social studies for three years. During that time, each of them had shared freely among themselves proven plans and strategies.

When Julie begins a brainstorming session on how to introduce a new unit, Joe and Janet jump in immediately with more ideas. Joe, Julie, and Janet do not consider competition a component of the working relationship. Their trust level is high as they share their successes.

With a governmental change in their state and a school board ready to get on board for the next school year, Joe, Julie, and Janet's district was in the process of considering a new system of "merit pay." Though dressed up with a new title and presented as a fresh possibility for better test scores, some teachers questioned their district's decision.

Janet, for example, saw the writing on the wall immediately. The words of her grandmother, "A rose is still a rose," came to mind. She immediately expressed her concerns to the team, which had stayed late one evening to do their lesson plans together. Over the pizza they had ordered, Joe put the question to the team. He asked them who would break from the pack first for the advantage of a higher salary, and what would happen to the two left in the dust?

More importantly, how would breach of the trust that their team had enjoyed so consistently affect their students? What would that do to the atmosphere on their wing? Looking at the bigger picture, how would this potential change impact the spirit of community in their school?

Big Valley Middle School, though a large facility, enjoyed a sense of community that was ideal. Joe, Julie, and Janet felt the support and closeness of a small team, as did many other groupings in the building. Their principal, Matt Start, instilled the spirit of sharing and support in the school staff and encouraged cooperation and mutuality. He too wondered how the new program and pay arrangements would impact what he had worked so hard to build.

Joe, Julie, Janet, and Matt did not want to work in a competitive corporate atmosphere. They believed that the pressures of "merit pay" would only bring division, resentment, and callous competition into an environment of cooperation and contentment. As the trio enjoyed their giant pepperoni-and-pineapple pizza, Matt stopped by their work area to get a sense of what they were thinking about the new program.

The team told their principal that as teachers they had concerns because they saw the merit system as a threat to what they had worked hard to develop. Even more so they spoke from their hearts, not only as educators but as parents as well.

Julie began by suggesting that though test scores gave an indication of student performance, they did not show the whole picture. Janet explained that when her daughter, Dora, now four, begins at Big Valley Elementary, she wanted her to benefit from the unquantifiable factors in education. Rather than being assigned a teacher set squarely on a salary hike, Janet shared that she wanted Dora to work with a teacher who treated her child with kindness and offered her support.

Joe interjected that as a parent he has appreciated teachers taking the time to communicate with him about his son Peter's progress in fourth grade. Julie added that she wanted to be included as a team member at her son Sam's school. It mattered to her that she relate with people who "know their stuff" as opposed to encountering "know-it-alls" on their way to the big bucks.

Matt agreed that such teacher traits are difficult to measure, and he would find it hard to rate teachers for pay bonuses based on quantitative data alone. When Joe offered him pizza, he knew that this action was only a gesture of goodwill and not an effort to gain approval or rank in a rating system. Simple human graciousness and cooperation keep the lines of communication open at Big Valley Middle School. Would this atmosphere continue?

Certainly the development of trust and growth of interpersonal relationships in a school do not show up on scores sent to the state. Yet somehow, the affective affects the hearts, souls, and minds of an entire school community. An atmosphere that places people first above competition and self-glorification brings success and deep gratification to all involved in the business of education.

THE INTERNAL CHANGES AND PERSONAL LOSSES THAT STEM FROM UNETHICAL ACTIONS

Film and literature describe the effects on the lives of those who choose, for whatever reason, to give in to pressure in job circumstances. A work of American literature, *The Devil and Daniel Webster* (Benét, 1965) tells of a fictitious New Hampshire farmer, Jabez Stone, who, due to misfortune in his work and sickness in the family, became discouraged.

For a promise of a change in his lot, Stone sold his soul to the devil, Mr. Scratch. Along with prosperity and fame, Stone experienced loss of peace, lack of independence, and fear. Being put in the situation of owing allegiance to the devil, Mr. Jabez Stone ultimately felt heartsick, distracted, and hopeless.

Realizing that he had entrapped himself in his deal with the devil, Stone enlisted a lawyer, Daniel Webster, to free him from his agreement. Webster, being a wise and clever man, approached the judge and jury involved in this unique case by making note of the positive commonalities all humans share. He also exhorted the value of freedom and explained that on the human journey one can become "tricked and trapped and bamboozled" (Benét, 50).

Yet according to Webster, being human also included pride as well as sadness. By giving a description of the journey of life, Webster renewed in the judge and jury their own sense of dignity as persons. Webster was no match for Mr. Scratch and eventually won Stone's freedom.

What might this American short story teach teachers and others working in a school? This tale sends the message to be your best self, to accept your strengths and weaknesses against a group or system that may want to draw you in, wear you down, or demoralize your ideals.

Educators, like the characters in the film and story, journey through the ups and downs of this sojourn called life. They too meet the temptation to succumb to discouragement, trickery, and sadness. Yet, each person working in a school has the option to choose the path of human dignity, the high road.

When presented with options incompatible with optimal character, after thought and consideration, all educators have the capacity to ignore any negative power in the workplace and to choose freely to be their best. All have the ability to speak and act with truth and integrity in all their dealings and interactions.

SUMMARY

Pressure presents educators with the option of responding as their best selves or going with the easiest or most expeditious option, though it is wrong. When faced with the temptation to cut corners, do personal business on school time, or neglect the job for unimportant personal priorities, teachers with ethical standards know what to do.

Schools with "merit pay" can challenge the patterns of group cooperation and sharing developed by teams who put their whole selves into developing plans together for the benefit of students. Some teachers may then face the option of selling out for material gain.

REFERENCES

Benét, S. V. 1965. *The devil and Daniel Webster*. New York: Holt, Rinehart and Winston.

Kozel, J. 2005. *The shame of the nation: The restoration of apartheid schooling in America*. New York: Crown Publishers.

Swank, H., Durning, T., Morales, N., Levine, D. (executive producers) and La Gravenese, R. (director). 2007. *Freedom writers*. Hollywood: Paramount Pictures.

CHAPTER 7

When Teachers Experience
Accusations of Misconduct

Mimi, a playful and attractive junior high school student, enjoyed her classes and teachers. She found drama and art among her favorite subjects because it was when she was engaged in these activities that she found it easy to freely express herself. When she went to science class it was a whole different atmosphere.

Mr. Jake Collins, a man in his 40s, had been a science teacher in his district for 23 years. He and his wife Pat moved to the western region of the country to enjoy the outdoors and climb mountains. They had grown to love the people and atmosphere of the west and found that country life suited them perfectly and afforded them a wholesome atmosphere in which to raise their two children, Bobby and Kate.

Mimi sat in science class watching the clock. The lesson about lifeforms too small for her to see bored her completely. Her mind wandered to the fun that she was having in drama class. Would she get the role of the young maiden in the old-fashioned horror show the class was putting together? Would a teacher like Mr. Collins even understand her world of drama? What was so great about things seen through a microscope? She would never know. To Mimi, science class was so very boring.

When class ended, Mimi Fontaine filed out with her classmates, eager to get on with something a little more interesting. As she was walking out the side door of the school, she reached into the pocket of her pink fleece jacket for her lip gloss, which she always kept on her key chain. Now it was missing. Perhaps she had dropped the small purple cylinder by her desk in the science room.

Mimi returned to her science classroom to find Mr. Collins writing tomorrow's outline on the board. That was another thing that bored her about the class. Everything was so organized. Mimi thought sure that Mr. Collins was clueless about spontaneity. Looking under her desk and around the room, Mimi spotted a purple object on the floor in the storage closet. Perhaps she had dropped the gloss when she'd helped put away the microscopes.

Mrs. Amelia Franklin, mother of an honor student, came to school to see Mr. Collins as her daughter, Jennifer, had stayed home for the last three days with the flu. Mrs. Franklin's goal was to keep Jennifer on the honor roll, so she contacted Mr. Collins about makeup work. Jake Collins told her he would slip the assignment into Jennifer's text and leave the book on his desk for her to pick up after school.

Mr. Collins had followed Mimi around in order to help her find the lip gloss. While in the storage area, Mimi mentioned that she recalled using the lip gloss during her drama class and thought she had also used it in science class as well. The conversation then turned to the events occurring in her drama class. Effusive and enthusiastic, Mimi began to share her ambition to play the role of the young woman. She told her science teacher that as this character she could become melodramatic, and in the words of her drama teacher, she could go overboard expressing fear and trepidation.

Facing Mr. Collins, in playful spontaneity and a quiet voice, Mimi began to tickle her teacher on the back of the neck as she described the tingles that would go up and down the spines of the audience. At that moment, Mrs. Amelia Franklin entered the classroom. What she saw from the vantage point of the teacher's desk was the hand of a female student tickling the back of Mr. Collins' neck.

What she heard were low voice tones from a young female student facing him. They appeared inches apart, and she was appalled to see them at such close range in the storage closet. In shock, Mrs. Franklin slipped the text into her canvas bag and left the room.

Mimi thanked Mr. Collins for his interest in her drama class and headed for home. Once the student had left, Mr. Collins returned to the front board and finished writing the outline. Once that was completed, he sat down at his desk and began to correct papers.

Grabbing a bottle of water from the right side of his desk, Jake Collins noticed that the text set out for Jennifer Franklin's mother was missing. It struck him as strange. Of course, having the ambition to be in a silly melodrama was strange to him as well. He put his attention back to correcting papers as the position of the sun indicated that evening approached, and he had promised to hike the path behind their log home with his son Bobby. One small stack of lab sheets to go and he could jump into his 4 x 4 and head home.

A week passed, and by this time Jennifer Franklin felt well enough to return to school. She caught up on her science assignments since, for her, things had returned to normal. Amelia Franklin, however, did not have any sense of resumption to normalcy. When she had downtime, she repeatedly reviewed in her mind what she had observed in the science room storage closet. She believed that what she saw was improper and wondered if Mr. Collins was behaving with this student in an entirely unprofessional manner.

Since Mr. Collins taught Jennifer, Amelia wondered if her daughter was safe in his class. Then it hit her. She now knew how to handle the situation. In the context of asking the principal if Jennifer could be transferred to Mrs. Binghamton's science class, she would tell Mr. Jefferson exactly what she saw.

Jean Lang, administrative assistant to Mr. Jefferson, arranged an appointment for Mrs. Franklin for the following day. Jean wondered what this meeting would be about. Jean Lang speculated that it might be worth eavesdropping on this meeting, as in the past she had heard some real tidbits out of Amelia by leaving the door of the principal's office slightly ajar.

When Mrs. Franklin arrived the next day for her 10:30 appointment, the administrative assistant decided not to take a break. If her instincts were correct, Amelia had a real tale to tell Mr. Jefferson. True to form, Jean Lang left the door open a crack. What she heard was truly shocking.

Jake Collins acting inappropriately with Mimi Fontaine? To Jean, this was the stunner of the season. She could not wait to tell Margaret Benson over at the high school. Being in a similar position there, Margaret offered Jean a few bits of news now and then. However, Margaret never came up with anything quite like this.

One's imagination could take this story down the path of serious false accusations for this completely innocent teacher. This scenario brings about consideration of how staff will treat the teacher once such accusations break. It also sets up the challenge to anyone reading this book to consider how an experience of false accusations would impact your career and personal life. How would you respond to and recuperate from such an affront?

RESPONDING TO A COLLEAGUE FACING SERIOUS ETHICS ALLEGATIONS

As in the case of Jake Collins, when the news breaks that a person of high regard, a teacher perceived positively by peers, faces allegations of improper behavior with a student, jaws will drop. Anyone knowing a teacher accused of impropriety with a student will respond with shock and even indignation. Team members and colleagues may experience a range of emotions, questions, and confusion.

When considering the possibility that a teacher known by many becomes singled out due to allegations of improper conduct with a student, think about personal reactions and responses. Following are considerations for those who work closely or have become acquainted with this teacher.

1. *Determine your original opinion of the teacher.* Perhaps an initial gut reaction indicated that this person has been falsely accused. Recall experiences with this teacher, conversations you have had with the person on various occasions, and the general impression in the school and district of the person. Note if you have an overall positive impression of the person.

    Remember times when you have discussed school issues and concerns, recalling his eye contact, mannerisms, and sense of dedication. Bring to mind memories of her genuine interaction with you relative to job or personal interests.

2. *Address your doubts.* Certainly they will surface. Rather than engaging in general gossip and chatter that may occur around this topic, express your questions in a journal or with a confidant, not for the purpose of getting involved with the rumor mill, but in order to process your perspective. Do you feel suspicious, concerned about the fragility of your own professional reputation, or insecure about relationships with parents or administrators?

3. *Give the person the benefit of the doubt.* It is not up to you or your colleagues to decide the innocence or guilt of a peer. The legal process will address that in due time. Once you have determined to be objective and withhold judgment, that decision will enable you to speak with staff, students, and parents with clarity and prudence.

4. *Be sensitive to all involved in this difficulty.* A teacher and his or her family are not only going through a legal trial but also are being tried in the court of public opinion and are enduring a severe personal trial. Relatives and friends, near and far, experience shock waves and pain from allegations of this magnitude.

   The student as well has gone down a path that has caused serious discussion and potential destruction to many lives. If a young person has brought about an accusation or created a story for attention, he or she has also indicated personal problems that need to be addressed. The family of the student involved carries a serious burden as well.

5. *Treat all involved with dignity.* Extend respect and consideration to all involved. Weigh and measure your words when the topic comes up so as not to become involved in slander of any kind. Do what you can to help the person you believe in and his or her family to retain their sense of self-respect and personal dignity.

6. *Support the teacher.* This can be done by simply withholding public judgment or becoming more involved as you feel comfortable. If the teacher had experienced another sort of tragedy, staff would send cards and notes, bring food, and offer to help drive children to their activities. Depending on how well you know the person, respond accordingly.

   You may wonder if the person is guilty and worry that your expression of certainty that he or she is innocent will make you appear to be duped. It may seem the same as not wanting a student to get by with lying to you.

   If you feel uncomfortable expressing certainty of the teacher's innocence, then, when you have an opportunity to communicate with the person, acknowledge your concern about the great difficulty he or she is experiencing and wish him or her well in a general way.

7. *Put yourself in their shoes.* Imagine yourself innocent of allegations, suddenly put on a leave of absence. You feel fearful of losing

the opportunity to teach again, needing to support a family, and being the center of unwanted attention.

Imagine yourself guilty of the same, having responded to an impulse of the moment or dealing with a dark secret, feeling remorse and regret, having to face those who trust you with the truth of a serious indiscretion and wrong action. Either way, your thoughts and prayers would be best directed toward the well-being of this colleague in such dire circumstances.

With thoughts of empathy for the teacher who allegedly treated a student in an unsuitable manner, any teacher may wonder how to avoid such a challenging situation themselves. Often many teachers just go about their day, dealing with the many details that come to them. Their minds are full of thoughts of assignments, curriculums, schedules, and meetings.

Questions abound concerning whether a deadline can be met, if lesson plans will be finished and turned in as expected, or if the room will be in good order for the Parent-Teacher Association meeting. Then too there are parental concerns. Does Jimmy have the aptitude for an advanced reading program? Could Megan be tested to determine if she has a learning disability?

Also on the mind of teachers are the avoidance of undue legal challenges and even the allegations of improper behavior with a student. Michael Simpson of the National Education Association's Office of the General Counsel noted some highlights in NEA's pamphlet *Teach but Don't Touch* (2007). Following are helpful suggestions for teachers in that regard:

> If possible, never be alone with a student—not in a classroom or a house, and especially not in a car. Never give a student a ride home. If you can't avoid being alone with a student at school keep the door open and stay in plain sight.
>
> Always maintain a professional demeanor and distance. That means no flirting, teasing, or joking about sex. Don't give gifts, unless you give one to every student, and don't single out any one student for special attention or flattery. Never send e-mails, text messages, or cards to students unrelated to school work, and don't ask students about their social lives or comment on their personal appearance.

Physical contact is a particularly tricky area. Younger children often seek out and need physical comfort from their teachers. In the early elementary grades, an occasional hug is probably OK. But as a general rule it's best to avoid most forms of physical contact especially kissing, hair stroking, tickling, and frontal hugging. And use common sense: a "high five" to acknowledge a job well done is fine; a slap on the bottom is not.

Nip crushes in the bud; never allow a student to obsess over you. While crushes can be flattering, they also can be fatal. An unfulfilled fantasy can result in a student acting out to gain attention or retaliating for being ignored.

If a student expresses a love interest, respond with an unambiguous "no." Don't equivocate and certainly don't encourage the student by acting pleased by the attention, It's also advisable to share this information with another adult and your union representative. In some circumstances, it may be appropriate to tell your supervisor and ask that the student be transferred.

But even if you follow this advice, there's no guarantee that you won't be the victim of unfounded charges. If the unthinkable happens, remember this: Never give an oral or written statement to school officials without first consulting with your union representative. Even innocent statements can be misconstrued. (Simpson, 2007, p. 22)

Going back to the fictitious story of Jake Collins, it appears that he is heading for serious trouble. His life as he knows it will change quickly and dramatically. Have you ever had someone make up a story about you or accuse you of doing something you did not do, even as a child? How have you responded to false allegations? How did you recuperate from the damage that those false accusations brought you?

When the allegations are of a public and legal nature, there is difficulty ahead for a teacher. It is important to know how to respond in such circumstances. In addition to legal assistance, how might a teacher survive it?

RESPONDING TO FALSE ACCUSATIONS

1. *Deal with the gossip and petty talk in the school community.* A teacher in these circumstances likely has been temporarily removed from his or her post. When aware that the allegations are

a topic of discussion, it is as important for the teacher to know that besides the fact that the content of the talk may be speculative or even malicious, it may also be supportive. However, what matters is not what others say, but what is actually true.

2. *Know that your actions are being observed but that your innocence is a clear reality.* When talking to those you know, be yourself, give good eye contact, and assume the body language of one who has nothing to be ashamed of because you are not guilty of wrongdoing.

   A teacher falsely accused can learn much from the words of the philosopher Socrates. He was accused as was stated at the time in Athens "of corrupting the young and not believing in the gods in whom the city believes but in other new divinities" (Grube, 1981, p. 29).

   Plato describes how Socrates presented himself under the circumstances. "From me you will hear the whole truth, though not, by Zeus, gentlemen, expressed in embroidered phrases like theirs, but though spoken at random and expressed in the first words that come to mind, for I put my trust in the justice of what I say, and let none of you expect anything else" (p. 24).

3. *Directly assure your family and friends of your innocence.* Share the situation as it occurred in a matter-of-fact and clear manner. Explain that you appreciate support, but give them the time, space, and option to respond to your situation as they are comfortable. Such legal issues bring out the vulnerabilities and fears of others. Once those in your corner are clear on how they wish to respond to your situation, they will be more likely to walk steadily with you the whole way.

4. *Learn to accept suffering.* Everyone goes through difficult times in life, and often we do not have the option of choosing the form it takes. Those who have experienced the sudden death or illness of a loved one, an accident or personal illness, and various losses and tragedies will confirm that fact.

   Lawyer and deacon Carl Cleveland went to prison, and in his words ultimately "the Supreme Court had decided my case in the quickest decision in U.S. history, but more significantly it had unanimously set aside my conviction. The court reasoned that what I was charged with was not a crime at all" (Cavins and Pinto, 2002, p. 56). Yet when in prison Mr. Cleveland learned to deal with suffering.

Describing his perspective after reading some psalms and the *Barclay Commentary on the Psalms*, he wrote in a newsletter to his family and his friends as follows: "The realization that there is a purpose in my suffering, perhaps even a great and as yet unseen purpose, has empowered me to take heart. Hope has returned. Faith is rekindled. Some brief moments of joy peek out through the dark clouds. In closing remember that you need not cry for me. My suffering is a natural part of life that I will embrace" (p. 45).

Those who have experienced trials in life attest to the fact that they do come and go and that with an attitude of hope, one is able to move through difficulties and come out a more mature person of deeper insight into life and the human condition.

5. *Trust your process and path.* When one is going through dark times, it is sometimes hard to see the light. However, many have gone though struggles and at the end could look back and see how they grew through a particular ordeal. Somehow in some way, one's life experiences and the insights and growth yielded from them link to the ability to address the events around the next bend on the journey.

6. *Read biographies of those who showed courage in the face of adversity.* The voices of historical and contemporary figures bring support and understanding in ways that flesh-and-blood friends may not be able to supply since they have not trod the same path you are taking.

7. *Seek the perspective and wisdom of others.* Whether you seek out a legal counsel, pastor, union representative, therapist, relative, or good friend, find a way to gain perspective and wisdom throughout the difficulty. Select a team of insiders who will go to bat for you at every turn. Work with them and allow them to help you stay strong.

REGAINING YOUR REPUTATION

Once a person has been cleared of a false accusation, he or she then has to find a way of reentry into the ordinary circumstances of life. A teacher who has been down the road of legal hearings or a trial hopefully experiences the clearance of criminal charges through the admission of the accuser or the perspective of a jury.

Some will say they "knew it all the time. This teacher would never have done such a thing." Others will have gone their own way or kept their distance, uncertain of what to believe or how to act in the presence of someone whose name has been damaged, though temporarily. It may take time for some to catch up.

The teacher who has been cleared certainly deserves reinstatement in the profession. However, for various reasons, the teacher may choose to go down another path. This person may find that entering a classroom would bring to the surface too many negative triggers on a daily basis.

For the person fresh from such a traumatic experience, memories of the chain of events would hang over him or her like a cloud. Consequently, this professional may want to use his or her talents in another field and would in fact find it refreshing and energizing to find a new life in another career.

With time, inner conviction, and new successes, a teacher who has endured and come through a false accusation deserves the healing that comes from the respect, congeniality, and care of colleagues. Teachers, family, administrators, and other staff members can do a lot to restore a broken colleague by treating him or her as a normal member of a school faculty.

If a teacher returns to school, he or she deserves the chance to get back in the groove. No doubt a casual discussion of the staff bulletin or a computer question would be more valuable in some respects than continuous questions of how things are going and what it was like to be falsely accused. Open acceptance and treating the teacher in a natural and matter-of-fact manner bring a teacher who has been through such a serious difficulty back into a staff community in a way that is comfortable for all involved.

SUMMARY

When hearing of accusations of sexual misconduct made about someone you know, it is always shocking. Teachers do not always know how to respond. They do not always realize either how to avoid getting into uncertain circumstances that could lead to misinterpretation. Knowing what to do when accused is hardest of all. Following that is the process of rebuilding one's life. All of these aspects of the accusation process can be addressed in ways to help others and oneself if ever in such difficult and precarious circumstances.

REFERENCES

Cavins, J., and Pinto, M. 2002. *Amazing grace for those who suffer: My thorn in the flesh*. Westchester, PA: Ascension Press.

Grube, G. M. A. 1981. *Plato: Five dialogues*. Indianapolis: Hackett.

Simpson, M. D. 2007. Falsely accused. *NEA Today* (January), p. 22.

CHAPTER 8

Decision Making for Students:
The IEP Process

Marcus, an eight-year-old boy, has just arrived from Guatemala. Although his parents cannot speak English, they are able to find a nearby elementary school and register him in second grade.

After working with Marcus for a couple of months, the second-grade teacher is concerned. She reports that Marcus is extremely shy and withdrawn and has some language issues. He does not participate in any group activity, never asks questions to clarify or seek more information, and often talks to himself. He has no friends, and during playtime he plays by himself in a corner of the room. She thinks that Marcus may have a language disorder. His parents agree that he should be assessed by the speech pathologist. While a speech pathologist does come to this school once a month, the school does not have any interpreter services for students like Marcus.

The speech pathologist is concerned about the assessment process because she can't involve Marcus' parents without an interpreter. Without family input, she cannot be sure that Marcus' difficulties are not a result of his lack of familiarity with the English language. In light of this, she reconsiders her assessment and decides that Marcus might benefit from reading interventions. She knows that the resource teacher in this school is awesome and does a great job with second- and third-grade students with learning needs. The speech pathologist submits a diagnosis of language impairments for Marcus, without making herself aware of the language needs of this student.

Even today, the speech pathologist thinks about Marcus and knows that perhaps it was not her best decision. A lack of resources should not have guided her decision making to such an extent. She knew that Marcus was not from an English-speaking background, and she knew that as an eight-year-old child he was at a critical age to establish literacy and social skills at school. She knows she should have engaged in fact-finding for a little longer period of time. She should have built a case for interpreter services. She should have made an effort to involve Marcus' parents in the IEP process.

This example demonstrates how many students may not receive the services they need because the stakeholders have not engaged in an ethical decision-making process. Ethical decision making is a process that puts the needs of the student first and is the key to success for the student with special needs.

The purpose of IDEA (Individuals with Disabilities Education Act, 2004), the federal law that governs special education in the United States, is to provide an appropriate education for students with special needs. This intent can be met only if members of the IEP team are committed to making meaningful decisions. It is important that students like Marcus receive prereferral interventions before their teachers refer them to a special education classroom. It is equally important that the results of prereferral interventions are analyzed before the general education teachers decide to take that next step. To do this requires that IEP team members access relevant information and engage in a cost-benefit analysis of their various options. It also requires that all stakeholders in the process—parents, the child if appropriate, psychologist, general educator, special educator, and speech pathologist—are involved in the process of decision making.

WHAT IS DECISION MAKING AND HOW DOES IT OCCUR?

Decision making is a cognitive process that leads to a course of action by analyzing and evaluating various options. Every decision-making process must produce a result that is effective, feasible, and beneficial to the student. The process usually begins when we need to do something but we are not quite sure what, how, and when. Therefore, this process begins with some level of reasoning and an analysis of facts.

During interactions in the IEP process, the various decision-making styles of the participants appear. As they make decisions, some members of the IEP team are guided by thinking, whereas others are guided by feelings; some lean toward intuition and others toward facts. Throughout the process of working with these different decision-making styles, it is important that the IEP process remain logical, analytical, objective, and fair toward the student.

In developing an IEP, it is important that the process shows the following:

1. *Ensure transparency.* Each person involved in the decision-making process must be familiar with the IEP process. The decisions should be made publicly, especially with regard to the people who are affected by it, such as the student and the parents.
2. *Avoid harmful effects.* Any potentially harmful effects the decisions may have should be carefully reviewed and shared with the IEP team. For example, if the student will be prevented from participating in gym class due to physical disabilities, the IEP team should discuss the pros and cons of this decision. By discussing these effects openly, the IEP team may be able to find a way in which these side effects or harmful effects can be avoided.
3. *Enhance fairness in the process.* The IEP team should consider whether a placement decision is regarded as fair by everyone affected by it. The members should weigh the benefits of various placement options before viewing any option as the only option for the student. The IEP team should come out of the meeting thinking that they have approached the best possible decision for the student and their decision will contribute to the success of the student.

ESSENTIAL COMPONENTS OF DECISION MAKING

As mandated by IDEA 2004, the complexity and diversity of decision making require a team review process that will ensure that special education mandates are addressed appropriately: that the IEP team members have a thorough understanding of the student's needs, as well as the knowledge and skills needed to make responsible decisions. Too often, *responsible* decisions are replaced by *convenient* ones. When the IEP team becomes involved in discussions about the availability of services at the school rather than focusing on the fact that those services are needed by the student, it is a sign that the decision making has become meaningless for the student. It is important to stick to the following steps to make responsible decisions.

1. *Analyze the facts.* The IEP team must focus foremost on the needs of the student, not the availability of services in the school. It is also essential that the IEP team members consider all relevant information in making their decisions. If relevant information is missing, the team must acquire that information before making their decisions.

2. *Analyze the context.* It is important that the IEP team discuss the context and services: the physical, instructional, social-behavioral, and collaborative dimensions of the proposed setting and how conducive that setting will be to providing the services the student needs.

3. *Document the decision-making process.* The IEP team should carefully document all discussions, describing the process used and the factors discussed in reaching a placement decision that will assure the child's advancement toward annual goals and objectives, involvement and progress in the regular curriculum, and education and participation in the least restrictive environment possible.

4. *Evaluate the decision-making process.* The IEP team must include an evaluation plan that examines the process of decision making itself so that recommended supports and services can be monitored for progress relating to the IEP goals and objectives for the student. The IEP team must monitor how many team members contributed to the decisions; how the decisions of placement, supports, and interventions have worked out for the student; and what changes need to be considered in the decision-making process for making better decisions for this student.

PARTICIPANTS IN THE DECISION-MAKING PROCESS

According to IDEA, specific individuals must be involved in the creation of an IEP. Each team member brings important information to the IEP meeting and must share information and work together to successfully write the student's IEP.

First, a school system representative should be present to interpret the child's evaluation results. Parents contribute valuable information about their child and should always be encouraged to attend. The special education teacher can ascertain the meaningfulness of special education placement, while a general education teacher can evaluate the ways the student might participate in the least restrictive environment. And finally, speech pathologists, occupational therapists, and other related services personnel should attend if specific related services are needed for the student.

Generally, each team member is responsible for the information that he or she brings, information that adds to the team's understanding of the student's needs and of the appropriate services. Since a meeting to write the IEP must be held within 30 calendar days of deciding that the child is eligible for special education and related services, these school personnel must make a sincere effort to ensure that all the necessary people are participating in the IEP decision-making process if it is to be completed in a meaningful and timely manner.

FACTORS TO CONSIDER IN THE IEP PROCESS

A meaningful IEP is not simply paperwork. It is a process that leads to a product documenting that the student is receiving a free appropriate public education that is consistent with all federal and state requirements. It summarizes the student's needs, goals, objectives, supports, services, and timelines toward those goals. It is a tool that is reviewed periodically and that guides the development of academic goals and expectations for the student for whom it was written.

It falls to the IEP team to ensure that all components of the specially designed IEP are implemented as described. To see how this might happen, let us analyze the relevant factors in the case of Marcus to determine how the process occurred. Here are the facts that we know about Marcus.

Student-related factors

- Marcus is from a non-English-speaking background.
- He is eight years old, a critical age for establishment of literacy and functional social skills at school.
- Marcus shows possible signs of a language disorder, but one has not yet been diagnosed.
- The school is not offering the best practice for English language learners.

External considerations related to the context of the school

- Marcus' parents do not speak English.
- Interpreter services are not available for parents, and the school has indicated that there are no funds for supplementary interpreters.
- The parents are not directly involved, creating a concern regarding informed consent for services for their son.

DO WE NEED ADDITIONAL INFORMATION OR FACTS?

The student-related factors and external considerations suggest that gathering the following information will help Marcus' IEP team make an informed and ethical decision:

- The IEP team does not have an accurate profile of the student's language skills and bilingualism at home.
- Marcus' parents must be involved in the decision-making process so that they can contribute valuable information regarding their son.
- It is important that the IEP team develop a good sense of the language environment and use at home and seek information from other districts (if they do not have resources in their own district) to understand how other districts are meeting the needs of English language learners.

While these facts are important, they are not enough to provide Marcus with an appropriate education. Facts by themselves only tell us what Marcus is currently experiencing; they do not tell us what ought to be happening for him to receive an appropriate education.

IEP TEAM BEHAVIORS: A COLLABORATIVE PROCESS

The development of the IEP is a collaborative process. Team members must collaborate to ensure that each student's educational experience is a success. To do this, all members of the IEP team must be viewed as equal partners, and their opinions must be valued and encouraged. They should engage in such positive team behaviors as offering meaningful suggestions, listening carefully, encouraging each other, and asking relevant questions. As members of the IEP team, parents are experts who have in-depth knowledge of and experience with the student. Parents should be actively supported and encouraged to participate in the planning and implementation process.

The IEP team members must focus on how to improve the school performance of the student. They should base their decisions on ongoing data on student performance collected over time and on student responsiveness to various educational interventions. They should consider which courses of action will produce the most beneficial outcome for the student, consider which option is the right (safe, compassionate, and responsible) thing to do, and make sure to look for similar cases that might offer potential solutions.

Research recommends that teachers develop relationships with parents and communicate regularly to build trust with them. During an IEP meeting, it is important to:

- Greet the parents;
- Introduce all the participants and explain their roles;
- State the purpose of the IEP meeting;
- Share positive observations about the student;
- Encourage parents to share information about their child;
- Provide time for a complete discussion without rushing through the meeting;
- Be flexible and a good listener throughout the meeting.

Before the meeting, gather as much information and facts as possible. Decisions may also be affected by school policies, so remember to examine the efficacy of policies in producing positive student outcomes. The worst examples of decision making are found when, in an IEP meeting, the team does not do what the parents are saying but record only what the school wants for the student.

DEALING WITH PRESSURE

Special education teachers may face barriers to providing appropriate education for students with special needs. For example, they may encounter parental resistance to an initial evaluation or placement or a disagreement on appropriate special education services with professional staff, parents, or administrators. The special educator may find herself faced with a choice between standing up for what she believes is an ethical decision for a student or agreeing to an opposite decision that is being pushed by parents or colleagues in the IEP team. What is the duty of a special educator toward students with disabilities when she faces opposition from others in the decision-making process?

When participating in the IEP process, always remember that you are there for the student. The principal may emphasize the lack of funds and resources available to provide services that you intend to recommend. The general educator may remind you of the school policy preventing you from making a decision about individualized instruction for the student. Other members of the IEP team may not see that the student really needs individualized instruction and can benefit from such instruction. When faced with conflicting positions, the best possible resolution comes through discussion with all relevant parties. Try to view this opposition as an opportunity to educate others in the IEP team. Practice your ability to showcase your recommendations with positive student outcomes. Illustrate how the other options may not lead to such positive outcomes for the student. Above all, keep the process fair and in good spirits.

Remember to have a spirit of mutual respect for all members of the team and to appreciate the work they have done. Such an attitude not only is important for your own peace of mind but also will encourage others who support the work of the team—the teachers, parents, and administrators who are participating in the meetings. Ensure that all team members have knowledge of the relevant laws, policies, and procedures and are aware of the obligations of the IEP team. To prevent

IEP team participants from coming with differing expectations, you may apprise them of this relevant information prior to the meeting. Try to resolve disagreements and hard feelings ahead of time.

Diplomacy is vital when you are handling the challenges that can surface during a meeting. Always remember that administrative support is a key factor in getting the best for the student. If you are responsible for calling the IEP meeting, engage in the following steps:

1. Schedule the IEP meeting at a reasonably convenient time for the parents. Inform them in writing, and offer the possibility of rescheduling for another time if necessary.
2. Inform the parents, in writing, who else will be at the IEP meeting and what their roles are. The parents may not be familiar with each professional's role in their child's life at school.
3. Ensure that all of the appropriate people have been invited to the IEP meeting. If you expect to discuss placing the student in an alternative setting, make sure a representative of that program attends the meeting.
4. Provide parents with the opportunity to bring an individual who is knowledgeable about the student's needs, and provide enough time for discussion. Encourage parents to ask questions of all the team members.

SUMMARY

Making good ethical decisions requires sensitivity to ethical issues and to the ethical aspects of the decision itself. To accomplish this, the IEP team should include all stakeholders who bring relevant information for making the best decision for the student. The team should weigh the options and choose a course of action that will benefit the student, not the setting.

Being ethical is not the same as doing "whatever the school accepts." Although many people in education strive toward standards that are, in fact, ethical, the standards in a given school may deviate from this ideal. For example, due to lack of resources, the IEP team in a specific school may be advised to keep all students in general education settings, even though a general education setting may not provide the best solution for certain students with special needs.

As an IEP team member you may encounter novel and difficult choices, and you may need to rely on discussion and dialogue with others to resolve those issues and dilemmas. Only a careful analysis of student needs will enable you to make sound ethical decisions about how to provide an appropriate education for your students.

CHAPTER 9

Testing

Mary had 20 students in her fourth-grade class. She really loved her job and thrived when she saw her students grow, but she was concerned about Sophia, a student who was a recent immigrant from Mexico. Sophia exhibited a variety of social, academic, and behavioral issues. She often doodled during class and did not respond to Mary's instructions. She had no friends, which was a sign as to why she had social issues. Mary had spoken to Sophia's parents about some of these concerns, but given the cultural differences between them, she was not sure if they had fully understood her.

After working with Sophia throughout the fall, Mary decided to initiate the special education referral process. She felt that Sophia needed more individual instruction than she was able to provide with 19 other students in her class. Sophia needed extra time to process math problems and had difficulty understanding some concepts. Mary wanted to make sure that Sophia received the best educational experience, but she found herself struggling. She shared her concern with Curt, the school psychologist. Curt suggested that Mary begin to document Sophia's behaviors and needs.

For the rest of the year, Mary documented Sophia's behaviors. At the same time, she set up expectations for Sophia and prompted her as much as she could. Her notes showed that Sophia did need individual instruction in math and reading. Mary thought it was time for a comprehensive evaluation of Sophia's reading and math skills. As part of the interdisciplinary team, she participated in the evaluation process as well as in the development of the Individual Education Plan (IEP) that followed.

The IEP team ascertained that Sophia had a specific learning disability in math and reading. Sophia also had social and behavioral needs. She needed to learn how to interact and communicate with peers and adults. The IEP team consulted the behavior specialist and suggested that a peer group be established where Sophia could interact with her peer role models and practice her social interaction and communication skills.

Mary was pleased with the IEP team's decision making. She knew that Curt, the psychologist, had done a great job of assessing and making a decision about Sophia's learning problems. Curt had experience working with students with diverse backgrounds. He had involved Sophia's parents in the assessment process and had used nonverbal culture-free tests to assess Sophia's IQ. He based this decision on information drawn from a variety of sources that included achievement tests, teacher recommendations, and parents' views.

Mary had worried how Curt would explain the test scores to Sophia's parents in the IEP meeting, but Curt did a marvelous job of informing the parents. In addition to special education services and supports, the IEP team discussed many possible instructional accommodations that would allow Sophia to benefit from her grade-level instruction in Mary's classroom. Although Mary did differentiate instruction and assessment for her students in class, accommodations targeted toward an identified learning disability were a relatively new concept for her. She knew that Sophia would be receiving services from Debbie, who was an excellent learning disabilities resource teacher. Debbie would also be the primary special education teacher responsible for implementing Sophia's IEP.

After reviewing the IEP, Mary set a meeting with Debbie. She wanted to gain specific information on how to apply the reading accommodations to ensure Sophia's access to the general education curriculum. Their meeting was helpful. Following the meeting, Mary felt that she had a better understanding of how to incorporate accommodations into her classroom. The IEP team had included a least restrictive environment (LRE) statement to monitor the accommodations for several weeks and then planned to meet again to assess how effective the accommodations were for Sophia.

Mary agreed that the suggested accommodations for Sophia were absolutely appropriate. Still, as the only teacher in her classroom, she *was not sure how she would manage to do all of this and still meet the needs of her other students. Although she differentiated instruction and assessment for all of her students, she soon found that making further accommodations for a child with an identified learning disability seemed to take a lot of her time.*

After considering the new situation, Mary sent an e-mail to Debbie, the special education teacher, hoping to get together and generate some ideas on how to develop the best learning environment for Sophia. Debbie offered to spend some time in Mary's class and assist in the implementation of accommodations. After a couple months, they had a parent-teacher conference to inform Sophia's parents about her progress. Sophia's parents were now involved in their daughter's education. The whole IEP team was working to ensure that Sophia was progressing!

As revealed in this case, all the stakeholders were involved in the IEP process and wanted to make sure that Sophia received the services she needed. There are many points of decision making in the process of IEP development. One of the most important is to collect information using a variety of assessment methods. If the psychologist or other evaluator(s) fails to use meaningful, reliable, and valid tools, the decision making will be affected.

Ethics are also an integral part of the instructional decision making. Teachers like Mary possess heightened awareness and are sensitive to the decisions they make. They are fully aware of the influence their decisions may have on the student's life, and they recognize that these decisions have ethical value, whereas many other educators have little idea about the ethical implications of their decisions. Decision making relies on meaningful assessments of specific aspects of student functioning in a particular context. It is important that teachers and other professionals working with students cultivate an awareness of the ethical implications of assessment.

ASSESSMENT: A PROCESS OF COLLECTING INFORMATION

Assessment consists of collecting purposeful information that assists in decision making. Teachers and other professionals involved in the eligibility decisions must remember that assessment leads to specific social and educational consequences for the student. Therefore, those who engage in the assessments that contribute to educational decisions should assume responsibility for the consequences. They should understand the meaning of the test scores and how that information is best used in the decision-making process.

While assessment is a useful tool in decision making, over the years testing has gained more notoriety than services for many children with disabilities. However, research indicates that educational interventions that are based on credible, reliable, and meaningful assessments are most beneficial for students with special needs.

Assessment helps provide information about student functioning, developing a profile of the student's needs, and clarifying how to better teach this student. Assessment is never perfect. It has errors and can suffer from subjectivity and bias. It is therefore especially important that educators involved in the assessment process be aware of these limitations of the assessment procedures.

IEP teams often face challenges when dealing with test scores and other information; the greatest challenge for them is to represent this information to the other IEP team members, including parents. Teachers have a tough time explaining the standard scores and grade equivalents to parents. It is important that teachers understand the scores and are able to explain the implications to parents.

Assessment for Special Education Decisions

There are two kinds of decisions that educators make for students with special needs: eligibility decisions and instructional decisions. In Sophia's case, the psychologist made the eligibility decision to use a culture-free test, which was appropriate as Sophia's primary language was not English. After the eligibility decisions were made, the IEP team faced the challenge of making sound instructional decisions for Sophia. They did a pretty good job of discussing the strategies that the special education teacher and general education teacher would use in reading and math instruction. They also decided how to best organize information so that Sophia could understand the concepts better.

Assessment for Systemic Changes

At the system level, administrators are faced with various other types of challenges with students in their schools. Many students do not feel ready to perform adequately on accountability tests. They may lack the motivation to perform, or they may not have mastered the skills. Students with disabilities often experience physical, social, emotional, or cognitive disabilities that prevent them from performing adequately on standardized tests.

Administrators are continually challenged with the need to respond to such issues as they collect assessment information to demonstrate that their schools are improving. In any circumstance, it is imperative that the administrators engage in ethical decision-making processes when responding to these challenges. They need to be fully prepared to explain why it is not ethical to involve students with significant challenges in the typical evaluation process and why it is important to engage in a good-faith referral process—one that is solely guided by the best interests of the student (in this case, the student with special needs).

Removing a student from a general education setting and referring a student to a self-contained classroom to raise school improvement ratings would not be considered a good-faith referral. On the other hand, failing to provide individualized reading and math instruction to Sophia would be viewed as unethical.

Instructing a parent of a student to keep the student at home during the state testing days so the student does not lower the school's scores is an unethical practice that unfortunately occurs in schools. Recently, in a school district close to one of the authors, a teacher and supervisor blew the whistle on a school superintendent who had instructed staff to take a group of students with disabilities on a field trip during the state tests so those students would not lower the school's scores.

EVALUATION AS AN ETHICAL PRACTICE

The American Evaluation Association (1994) provides a list of principles to guide ethical practice in evaluation.

1. *Engage in systematic inquiry.* It is important that evaluators engage in systematic, data-based inquires about whatever is being evaluated. If they need to know about the present level of functioning of a student, they must collect information from various sources. They should be fully aware of the psychometric properties of the instruments that they plan on using. They should have a clear idea about the measures that they will be using to evaluate the outcomes. They should have an idea of how they can use feedback to improve the processes and outcomes.

2. *Recognize the boundaries of competence.* Evaluators need to provide competent performance to stakeholders, and this may involve refusing to engage in activities in areas in which they are not competent. If they are not trained in the administration of IQ tests, they should not engage in this activity. If they have not had experience working with English-language learners, they should refrain from making decisions about such students. They should also engage in the continuing education processes to maintain high standards of performance.

3. *Show integrity in the process.* Evaluators must demonstrate honesty and integrity in the entire evaluation process. This requires them to refuse to engage in assessment activities that may be desired by a system but are not appropriate for a given individual. Only by refusing to use technically invalid tests can users push the developers to refine these tests. They should be willing to ask challenging questions.

4. *Show respect for people.* Evaluators must respect the confidentiality, dignity, and self-worth of the respondents, parents, teachers, and other stakeholders with whom they interact. Results of individual student performance should not be discussed informally among staff members. When working with young children, or populations of students with disabilities, or individuals who are unable to give consent, assessors should take special care to protect their interests.

5. *Know responsibilities for general and public welfare.* Evaluators should be careful about diversity of interests and values that may be related to the general and public welfare. They should remember the numbers generated by the testing process represent people. If the findings are based upon a small sample size, they

should make the public aware of the limitations of the results. They should engage in culturally sensitive evaluations and should adopt a culturally responsive practice in sharing data and results.

6. *Focus on accurate and thorough evaluation.* Evaluators must remove their own biases before conducting assessments. They should adopt a multimethod approach to evaluation and attempt to collect information from a variety of resources.

THE ADMINISTRATOR'S ROLE IN THE PROCESS OF ASSESSMENT

Administrators must ensure that they hire qualified candidates to conduct the tests. They must also provide ongoing support and training for evaluators and keep them both sensitive and effective. They should specifically be aware of the context-specific needs of their schools and be familiar with the kind and level of training evaluators will require in order to conduct culturally sensitive and effective evaluation.

They themselves should be knowledgeable about issues such as special education eligibility and due process, as well as have a general awareness about the psychometric and contextual issues of various test instruments, such as validity, reliability, standard error of measurement, and ethnic composition of the standardization sample. They should continually refine their evaluation systems to meet legal and ethical requirements.

Assessments should be fair to all students and have educational consequences that are beneficial. If unfair tests are used, decisions based on that test may not benefit the student. Achievement tests should be used only for accountability decisions after changes have been made in the curriculum, after which teachers can ensure that students have been taught the knowledge and skills on which they will be tested. Furthermore, it is essential that assessments be used in conjunction with other criteria if high-stakes decisions are to be made. No decision should rely on only one test.

ESSENTIALS OF APPROPRIATE TESTS/ASSESSMENTS

- The tests should yield reliable information and should demonstrate consistency in results.

- Tests should also be valid. Validity is the extent to which a test measures what it is supposed to measure. Although validity is a subjective judgment made on the basis of experience, several indicators are available to demonstrate various types of validity, such as content of the test, meaningfulness of the test, and predictability of test factors for various types of disorders.
- Testing should protect privacy. According to the Family Educational Rights and Privacy Act (FERPA) of 1974, student and family privacy are protected from inappropriate school decisions and actions. Teachers and psychologists should be careful to keep information confidential and should respect the individual's and family's rights.
- Testing should be comprehensive. In other words, evaluators should collect information from a variety of sources, such as observations, interviews, or teacher ratings, in addition to the standardized tests. When creating a comprehensive assessment plan, multiple measures and sources should be used.
- The test and the testing process should be fair. Evaluators should consider the age, native language, and ethnic background of the person who is being assessed and use culturally responsive assessment approaches for students from various linguistic and cultural backgrounds.
- Evaluators are obligated not only to select nonbiased test instruments and use them in a way that is not racially or culturally biased but also to seek parent involvement and interpreter services, if needed. The goal should be to gather the best information for making the best possible decision for the student.

TYPES OF ASSESSMENT

Assessment should be conducted at various points of time throughout a program and should include formative and summative assessment and quantitative and qualitative assessment. The goals/objectives of the program must guide the selection of assessment tools.

Formative and Summative Assessment

Formative assessment is conducted during a program, thus providing the opportunity for evidence for student learning in a particular setting or content area. The primary purpose of this type of assessment is to improve quality of student learning and instruction. This type of assessment leads to curricular and instructional modifications and provides progress data to make instructional decisions.

Summative assessment is used to check the level of learning or gains at the end of the program. Summative assessment at the end of the program provides information on whether students have met the program goals and objectives. Both types of evaluations are needed for making decisions about the long-term effectiveness of an educational program.

Qualitative and Quantitative Assessment

Quantitative assessment measures use numerical indices and enable educators to provide numerical evidence of student learning, while qualitative measures provide descriptive and contextual evidence in the form of narrative information or anecdotes that show student learning. Examples of quantitative assessments include comprehensive exams, standardized tests, surveys, and certification exams.

Qualitative assessments include portfolios, exit interviews, writing samples, and essays. Quantitative assessment generally focuses on a few specific questions over a large number of cases and provides broad, generalized information about the program. Qualitative assessment, because of its open-ended nature, produces more comprehensive, detailed information, but about relatively few cases.

It is important for educators to develop a sound knowledge base of assessment and apply appropriate methodology for evaluation. Educators need to know about the goals of assessment, outcomes they want to produce, and processes they engage in for making decisions.

SUMMARY

Every school in the United States uses some form of standardized assessment to measure students' academic progress. Despite much debate about the limitations of standardized testing and its appropriate use, assessment will continue to be used to indicate educational expectations, accountability, progress, and performance results for the students and teachers at school, state, and national levels.

It is therefore important that educators evaluate their own decision-making capacity from time to time. Every school engages in the process of decision making using assessment information. These include prereferral classroom decisions, entitlement or eligibility decisions, instructional decisions, and accountability decisions.

Educators must remember that all their decisions affect the lives of and long-term outcomes for the students and their families.

REFERENCE

American Evaluation Association. 1994. "American Evaluation Association guiding principles for evaluators." www.eval.org/Publications/Guiding Principles.asp.

CHAPTER 10

Showing Integrity When Working with Colleagues

Tanika sat in the seminar in amazement, thinking that the speaker had to be talking about the ongoing situations in both of her schools. As a special educator, Tanika worked in two different schools in her district. Because she had a master's degree that included training to work with children with cognitive impairments as well as those with behavioral problems, she worked to lend support to her colleagues in those buildings who did not have the breadth of her training.

What had this speaker said that had caught her attention so dramatically? Tanika thought the speaker, brought in for midyear training, was helpful but found her mind drifting a bit. Then the speaker stated, "You may have to compromise your desire to belong in order to do your job on principle." When Tanika heard these words she knew exactly what the speaker, a former special educator herself, meant.

In fact, just the previous week, when Tanika had been at River Hills School, she noticed that the teachers all wore hand-painted pins. They had just attended a baby shower for one of the third-grade teachers and had received the pins as party favors. Tanika had not been invited. She knew why. It was not only because she was not at River Hills full-time due to her commitment to Rivertown Middle School, but it was also because of her role at the school.

Most recently she had been involved in an IEP meeting about a student named Willie who had just been tested and found to have learning disabilities. When the team developed the IEP, Tanika suggested that the current reading program used by the entire district was not the best fit for this student.

Tanika believed that the student needed alternative strategies that she felt should be included in the IEP. The classroom teacher did not agree, and as a result Tanika respectfully expressed her opposition. Though Tanika treated her with calm and care during the meeting and the teacher, Mrs. Mayberry, came on board at the end of the meeting, things did not end there. Though Mrs. Mayberry expressed agreement to, in her words, "save face," she spoke harshly with Tanika later in the parking lot.

Mrs. Mayberry, who happened to be the host of the shower, purposely excluded Tanika from the event as an act of revenge. Mrs. Mayberry told Tanika that she had years of experience and reminded the special educator that, though she was fresh out of graduate school, she did not have the experience to trump her in public. Mrs. Mayberry's pride was deeply wounded, and she resolved to never forget it. She decided not to forgive Tanika for not falling in line with her way of thinking in terms of the kind of instruction Willie needed.

While the speaker continued on, Tanika's mind switched over to Rivertown Middle and another incident. Again she had to stand on principle and let go of any personal desire to belong in the inner circle there as well.

Tanika's lunch at Rivertown was from 12:40 to 1:10. During that time the only occupants in the staff lounge were four women who had taught together for decades. When team teaching grew in favor, these sixth-grade teachers banded together in a tight team. They knew one another well, had similar-aged children, and aimed to retire in the same year. In fact they even played golf as a foursome.

Before Tanika came to Rivertown, this group had the advantage of being the last staff members to eat in the lounge. Because no one else was there, they spoke freely with one another about their students, husbands, children, weekends, and personal lives. When Tanika began at the school, she was assigned to work with a sixth-grade girl, Amanda, who had each of the foursome for her instruction. Tanika took pride in doing her best for all of the students on her caseload.

When working with Amanda, she noted that the girl learned best when a teacher used visuals to bring dimension to the instruction. As it turned out, none of these teachers were big on the visual modality and often just talked to their students in a lecture style. Tanika took it upon herself during the first week to speak to them about Amanda's needs and to offer suggestions as to how the teachers could present their lessons so that Amanda could learn better.

The foursome operated as if they had one mind. None of them saw value in Tanika's input and basically ignored her suggestions. They also noticed that when Tanika came into their classrooms, she focused almost exclusively on Amanda. They believed that Tanika's time would be better spent assisting them with other challenging students who were not on IEPs. They felt she was wasting her time so engaged with Amanda.

In fact they believed that they had a harder job than she did and even asked her to correct student papers while she sat there by Amanda. In their minds, if Tanika could take the load off their jobs, they could get to the golf course sooner and really be a foursome. When Tanika explained that helping the teachers correct papers was not the reason she was in the room, it only created more resentment on the teachers' part.

When Tanika walked into the lounge the group gave her little attention. Though she had just as much of a right to be in there as it was her lunch period too, Tanika felt as if she was imposing. When the group complained to her about a student on her caseload, Tanika reminded them that it was her policy to speak about students in her office or in their classrooms. Tanika felt so much pressure, both professionally and socially, that she ultimately decided to eat alone in her office.

As time passed she fortunately found the company of a music teacher, Ed, also assigned to River Hills Elementary, who, like Tanika, found the lounge a difficult place to relax and unwind. The foursome found the music teacher a target for their complaints related to the school music program. Tanika and her newfound lunch colleague felt it was important to act professionally and put the needs of students first. Consequently they gave up full social acceptance in their schools in order to do what they believed to be best for students.

BALANCING BELONGING WITH PRESERVING PRINCIPLES

Teachers rejected for standing on principle find social acceptance in other areas of life. In order to maintain balance, they adopt a mind-set that says they go to school to help their students. They sometimes have to sacrifice popularity with the staff in order to accomplish goals set for students. As far as belonging goes, they know that school is a social entity but not necessarily the one where they will meet all their personal needs for socialization.

They choose after-school activities at a health club or church to meet individuals with other perspectives. They join professional organizations and cluster with other educators who believe as they do and form small groups to reinforce their educational philosophies and dedication to the field of education. They go to graduate school or take classes for professional and personal growth to maintain perspective and develop their expertise.

Many circumstances occur in the life of an ethical professional requiring her to go against the grain and stand on principle. One place where this can occur is at professional conventions. When principled professionals attend a convention paid for by their district, they plan carefully and determine what sessions to attend. They select those that will both help them grow and be in tune with their school district's current goals and needs.

Conventions offer luncheons and gatherings that mix socializing with professional exchanges. This is the wonderful part of such experiences. Teachers not only find fulfillment in networking but also have the opportunity to discuss a range of topics of interest to all involved. Teachers also find others from different parts of the state or nation with whom to maintain a long-distance correspondence relative to their jobs and also their lives.

One of the authors met a teacher on an elevator at a conference, and during a brief ride they discovered many commonalities. These teachers kept in touch for a few years, discussing professional and personal topics.

A teacher, Jane, told one of the authors during a meal at a conference that she felt that it was important to use her time well while attending the event. She did not believe that she should be mainly shopping or partying if her district paid her way. She personally felt responsible to "attend everything" and make the most of the experience.

To Jane it would have been a disservice to her employer if she didn't attend the sessions but just sat around or spent a lot of time shopping or going sightseeing. Jane also chose to stay until the last session of the day as opposed to leaving early to avoid heavy traffic. Jane planned and involved herself so that both she and her district gained a great deal from her conference attendance.

Sometimes teachers find themselves in unusual situations relative to conventions. One district's goal was to save money and at the same time open a conference opportunity to as many teachers as possible. When one of the authors arrived at the conference, she was asked by someone from her district to take a name badge bearing the name of another teacher and wear it for the day.

What the district had done was register certain people for a conference that lasted more than one day with the intention of sending a different group each day. For example, Sue Smith was to go for an entire day as Jill Jones. The author not only believed that was against conference policy but also would have been embarrassed being seen wearing someone else's name. Thus she had to face an ethical dilemma and confront the district personnel in this regard.

The hard part of many of the ethical challenges teachers face is that they appear to be relatively minor matters that come up unexpectedly. Teachers then must react quickly and do what they believe to be correct. It is often difficult to manage such situations that require split-second thinking. However, when an individual lives an ethical life out of habit, he finds his way to the right path in the various circumstances he meets.

DRESSING FOR ETHICAL AND PROFESSIONAL SUCCESS

Jane, mentioned in the previous section, also expressed her thoughts in regard to staff attire. Is there a way to dress ethically as well as professionally? According to Jane, some staff members come to school in trendy clothing that is inappropriate for professionals.

She was not referring to casual and comfortable clothing worn by teachers who work with students outdoors or whose roles require them to be on the floor or to restrain students with severe behavior problems. Certainly they cannot work comfortably in a suit or dress clothing. Jane was referring to staff members who wore outfits such as short or low-cut tops.

Some teachers mix up their messages. When dressed with dignity they send the message that they deserve to be treated with respect and that they respect their students. When coming to work in an outfit worn for clubbing or partying, they set the wrong tone. Instead of an educational tone, they move the venue from education to fun and games.

Teachers who want to be taken seriously present themselves as professionals by choosing attire appropriate to their positions. Teachers, aware of the value of raising the standards of the profession, know that as in the business world, they must look the part. A male teacher in a tie speaking to a dad coming from work in a suit sends the message that they are on equal professional footing. Female teachers whose skirt length is in tune with that of the parent express that they are about the business of education.

Some staff members believe that if they dress in the same fashion or styles as students, they will be better able to relate with them. An example of such a teacher has been called "Juvenile Judy" in a previous book by these authors, *Surviving Internal Politics within the School* (2006). This type of teacher dresses in "cool clothes" in the fashion of the day as defined by the youth culture.

> Judy believes that if she can blend in with her class, they will like her. She is certain that if they think she is really "with it," then she will have achieved success. However, administration takes notice of staff professionalism or lack thereof. Administrators and team members will have a challenge in supervising and working with Judy.
>
> Direct, clear, and consistent expression of expectations and desires, just as to a child is the means to attempt to reach the part of her that strives for developmental appropriateness. Official and unofficial mentoring will be of direct benefit to those who fall into the Juvenile Judy category, not only for the teacher's advantage but also for the benefit of student and families. (p. 146)

Teachers set the tone and culture of a building. By their dress they contribute to the atmosphere of a classroom. It is up to staff as to whether the culture is raised or lowered. They send an ethical message not only by who they are but also by how they present themselves.

SECOND-CLASS-CITIZEN STAFF

Like Tanika's experience in the fictitious example at the start of this chapter, some individuals, by the nature of their job roles, are relegated to the status of second-class citizens in their schools. Some strata of staff choose to see themselves as more important than others due to their level of education, the years they have worked in a building, the connections they have made with administrators, or the amount of money they make in their jobs.

Such staff members then choose to place themselves as first-class staff members and see themselves as better and more important in the work that they do. They view food services and custodial workers, paraprofessionals, and volunteers as less important. However, if they were without the support and the services that these individuals offer to the school, they might also be the first to complain.

Some teachers feel superior to other teachers because they believe that when they teach older students with more sophisticated and difficult subject matter, they themselves are superior to teachers who teach preschool, kindergarten, or early grades with foundational skills. Only on occasions when teachers do an official trade do those who believe they stand on the top of the pecking order realize that there are teaching skills specific to all levels that require training, skill, and creativity.

Some important staff members, even though they have less education than others, will choose to see substitute teachers or itinerants as less important because they are not around as much and are not "in the know" regarding staff inside information or even gossip. They see them as less valuable to the school and offer them little of their time.

Some schools give itinerant staff, though they are highly educated such as social workers, psychologists, or occupational therapists, less status as represented by the spaces they are allowed to use to do their work. They are provided with small, stuffy spaces that serve as closets, or noisy spaces with "paper-thin" walls. Spaces lacking privacy compromise the effectiveness of work built upon confidentiality.

Placing someone who works with small groups for tutorial and specialized teaching, requiring concentration on the part of the students, in a room adjacent to the student lunchroom minimizes the opportunity for students who need the help of the support staffer who works with them.

Service providers who travel from building to building need to optimize their time while in each setting. They are often unaware of the current issues in the many buildings they serve. A hospitable and accommodating environment helps them to settle in quickly and perform their jobs effectively for the benefit of students and the building staff as well.

Some staff fail to give a volunteer who may be a corporate executive or retired teacher the gratitude and respect he deserves for his efforts simply because he is not paid for his contributions. They refuse to acknowledge the life experience and training he brings to his volunteer work in a school.

No school district could function solely with any one group of individuals. A library clerk or the principal, a PhD in English, or a reading volunteer—all matter. Each has dignity. When treating all adults with respect, a school sends the message to students that they, in their diversity and variation of ability and talent, matter just because they are human beings.

WORKING ALONGSIDE UNETHICAL COLLEAGUES

Challenges come in schools when the social dynamics of the adults play out in ways that denigrate or harm others. In various educational workplaces, there are interactions that create drawbacks for those who are less able to deflect the negatives that come with them. A teacher can have high principles and good intentions but after a time, being close to others at school with less altruistic motives, can begin to feel that her personal standards could easily erode.

In some environments, various behaviors among the staff become the requirements for social acceptance. The majority who sets the tone of the adult culture may tolerate off-color jokes, bigotry, gossip, or inappropriate relationships among themselves. Setting this as the norm, those who find such behaviors and attitudes offensive can easily wear down and begin to want to "go along to get along."

However, those with true character balk at engaging in activities and talk that chip away at the dignity of individuals or groups. A joke about a certain minority group is not funny to those who choose to respect and value diversity. A snide or critical comment about a staff member or parent made one too many times might just be the one that will be confronted by an educator of principle.

Those who find the manners and values of their peers intolerable do reach the point of decision. In doing so they choose to disengage from the small groups they have determined to be detrimental to their own character, or they decide to respond to them directly.

Saying "Please do not tell me any more ethnic jokes as I do not find them funny" or repetitively not laughing as these jokes are told are ways to extinguish off-color humor. "I love and respect my [insert group being ridiculed] cousin. I have learned a great deal from his/her perspectives and experiences" could quickly put a hush on someone attacking a certain group.

One can be fully aware of the need to fit in and belong and yet choose to take the high road rather than sacrifice integrity. Those on the staff who know a genuine person when they see one have the option of coming along with the person of principle or following the crowd. Maybe the one time that a teacher with character speaks up for a higher value is the time that others will finally have the courage to do the same. Ethical leadership may be all they need.

Coming into a new setting can be a challenge for any teacher. It takes time to learn where to find materials, to know whom to ask for what type of information, to meet the families, and to know the staff. A new person on a faculty comes with certain expectations. Maybe initially the people he meets are helpful and respectful. That would be the expectation of any professional.

However, sometimes when a new person comes into a different staff configuration, he may eventually come upon unethical practices that challenge the general district code of ethics. It is at this point that he has to make choices.

Appealing to a higher law through modeling that code of behavior is certainly a way to begin. However, if various teacher behaviors such as lack of confidentiality, not fulfilling contractual expectations, or mistreating students occurs, a person with high standards will find it hard to stand by.

Certainly there is a boundary around a circumstance over which it is not appropriate for colleagues to cross, as it is already being addressed by supervisors. One can find that out through observation and have the certitude that he should not get involved.

However, as time passes and blatant ethical violations appear to go unnoticed, it is time for action. Finding someone of influence in a system with whom to confer is the ultimate step. Perhaps though the circumstances and an approach for presenting what has been seen, heard, or read could be discussed confidentially outside of school with a counselor or trusted associate or friend.

Once the perspective has been verified, a plan can be developed to ensure that things are going well in terms of staff performance and student and family respect. Such matters can be delicate and are best approached with wisdom and prudence.

ARE UNETHICAL COLLEAGUES ALWAYS "BAD" PEOPLE, OR ARE THEY ENGAGED IN SOME BAD HABITS?

When assigned to a school building, to a particular department or grade level, a teacher goes into her situation on good faith, with clear goals to offer her best professionally to help the students assigned to her. Colleagues who are not on the same path toward educational excellence present a major roadblock.

These individuals, for whatever reason, have character or behavioral deficits that impact a team or deprive students of the best education possible. Such circumstances make for a very difficult working environment. Are they necessarily morally corrupt people? Are they intentionally malicious?

Giving some staff members the benefit of the doubt, determining that no one can judge another without having lived the life of that person, the detriment that they do to a viewer can be reduced by seeing them through the lens of humor. Following are composites of types of teachers who interfere with the best that can be in a school.

Vicious Victoria

A snide remark, a curt comment, an antagonistic response, a mean-spirited remark here and there characterize this teacher. Is Victoria having a bad day? Does she have a challenging life experience that constantly puts a damper on her happiness? Is she in the wrong career? Does she have too few interests in life? Does she have an old hurt that remains unresolved?

Approaching Victoria gently with consistent kindness sends the message that she has nothing to fear. Her habits of barking back or snapping may remain, but she will have little cause to blame and attack a person of goodwill.

Climbing Claudia

A seeker of a high position in the district may appear to step on heads en route to the final destination, whatever that may be. Seemed indifference to students and building concerns, an air of detachment regarding the future of a department, a manner of superiority regarding peers—all could indicate that Claudia's eyes see a prize down the road that is not a part of her current work world.

Dressing as if she works at a national office or unlike those in her school may make peers feel uncomfortable. Hearing her talk about the content of her graduate classes might put peers into a mode of inferiority or insecurity.

Does Claudia intend to exclude those in her present situation? What else could be on her mind? Might she have a strong commitment to education that she believes she can best fulfill in another position for which she is preparing? Does the content of her classes interest her but not her peers?

Finding time to speak with Claudia may shed light upon her goals and plans. Maybe she has goals of purpose to benefit students other than direct daily involvement. Maybe she is moving forward for professional fulfillment. Only she can say.

Klepto Clem

Using school items and property for work or for home, slipping paper clips and rubber bands into his pocket, and taking home the school laptop without permission make one pause to notice. Does Clem take things home purposely, or does he just habitually put things into his blazer pocket, using such items indiscriminately? Who knows what agreement he has with the resource teacher relative to laptop use? If he damages school property used at home, won't he eventually be held accountable?

Learning if Clem is more of the absentminded professor–type absorbed with job detail would be helpful. If he is going beyond school policy in terms of what he takes, he may be held accountable at some point for overuse of materials or damage to technology that is not his. Time will tell.

Lying Lyle

Here is a teacher who appears to continually speak spontaneous lies to serve an immediate purpose. When asked to stay late to do lesson plans, he tells the team that his great-aunt died and he has to go to the funeral home. (Lyle has had several great-aunts die during the fall term.)

When asked to be on a committee for the fall festival, Lyle has so many other commitments already that it is impossible for him to do this, but he says he will help out at the function next year. Next year comes around, and Lyle is very busy with his Scout troop and cannot stay to help. On it goes. Lyle has a creative option to explain why he can or cannot do something relative to school.

Is Lyle that busy? Is his life that tragic? As a team, approach him seeking answers in order to seek his service. Does he need encouragement, confidence, or affirmation? Where do his skills fit best? Is he a serial master of verbal fabrications used to serve the moment, or is there some event, demand, or private priority behind his hedging? Concerned confrontation may offer the answer.

Backdating Nate

Getting the report in on time seems to be less important to Nate than giving the appearance of timely completion. Following state guidelines on paper as opposed to reality may matter more to Nate than presenting a true picture of his work.

Perhaps team members represent the process of an assessment or project according to reality, with the exception of Nate, who reports his progress according to legal expectation. An honest team who put forth their timelines with truth may face a minor citation. Mercy from those in charge of these results may cover their efforts and honesty. Those who review paperwork can count and certainly call into question what appears to be Nate's reworking of reality. The process will prove the results one way or another.

Enterprising Elmer

Sending an e-mail for his personal business from a school computer and checking home messages during class time on the school phone take from Elmer's student contact time. Ignoring district practice and placing his sense of urgency about business or his personal social life bring Elmer into question by some of his peers.

What is going on in his life that draws him to appear to put students second to his other interests? Does he stay late to catch up? Has he checked with administration regarding his dual focus?

Check with the building administration or union officer relative to policy regarding technology and phone use for personal activities. Maybe it is time to request that this be placed in the staff bulletin for everyone's, including Elmer's, clarification.

Religious Rex

Rex has lost sight of the fact that modeling values such as kindness and respect holds weight, even in an environment where separation of church and state is standard. To him, a subtle and sometimes direct effort to convert students to his brand of religion takes priority. Rex forgets that his zeal for converting others as expected by his church has to match the circumstances.

Though his district allows seasonally appropriate songs having religious themes and offers literature classes using writings from various religions, Rex deems it necessary to work at getting students to come to functions at his church. His goal is more than their attendance at a church-sponsored basketball game or a concert. If he can get them there, then he could bring them on board, in spite of the fact that their parents have signaled to the contrary, choosing to raise their children in other expressions of faith and values.

Rex does not understand his boundaries as a professional. Once Rex crosses the line, parents will catch on to his aims. Does he have good intentions in terms of the outcome of the youth of the school? Does Rex want his students to know the richness of his religious experience? Does Rex realize the richness in the spiritual lives of the families that already exist?

If Rex approaches a staff member at lunch, he may extend the invitation to attend an event at his church. A teacher curious about Rex's church community can certainly attend. A teacher who finds fulfillment elsewhere can politely decline, invite Rex to attend an event at his or her place of worship, or open a dialogue to find commonalities of belief and values and build a relationship from there.

MODELING ETHICAL BEHAVIOR—IS IT JUST FOR STUDENTS?

Certainly, students notice the behavior of their teachers. They notice the small things. They view consistent human values and certainly see failures. No professional is the paragon of perfection. Staff members come to work. They try their best. They relate as genuine persons as well as consistently caring and supportive professionals.

However, it is not just the students who see the dedication and concern of teachers and other educators. Being together in a school environment, working closely day in and day out, offers the opportunity for staff members to witness skills and strategies developed by their peers.

They see solid teaching going on all the time. They observe competencies they choose to emulate. They learn new approaches to presenting material. Staff members notice the courage and commitment of those with whom they share the vision of bettering the lives of students and families. The fullest good in one educator raises the bar for another.

Modeling the best of educational ethics and high regard for learning impacts the culture of a school. A school that seeks to operate to bring the best out of each young person and each educator in a school community raises the total culture of the educational section of society. When a school signals that it values each individual by taking full responsibility for outcomes and for students and staff reaching their full potential, not just as learners but also as people of character, an entire society benefits as well.

AIMING FOR ETHICAL SYSTEMS—THE CHARGE FOR ALL IN SCHOOLS

As one ethical educator impacts a single student or an entire class, so too does she influence a single family and also several families. An ethical educator creates the atmosphere of dignity and respect just by how she conducts herself and treats others. In so doing, she contributes to the creation of ethical systems.

Father Edward Malloy, CSC, president emeritus of Notre Dame and member of the University of St. Thomas Board of Trustees, stated the following at the dedication of McNeely Hall on that Minnesota campus:

> This wonderful facility—and the faculty who will work within and the students entrusted to their care—needs to be a place where character can be promoted. Those qualities that I identified have other names: like prudence, justice, fortitude and temperance—the so-called cardinal virtues. It goes under the presumption that if we want to turn out leaders of character, we need to foster certain attributes and prevailing values in and out of the classroom.
>
> My second point has to do with accountability. We know society has seen a hemorrhaging of respect and confidence both in the business enterprise and in the regulatory enterprise. Who's watching the watchers? How can we restore trust in corporate life? In the relationship between boards and those that they oversee? In the relationship between management and the workforce? In the relationship between institutions and the broader society that they work within and, in the end, serve?
>
> Accountability starts early, in the relationship between parents and children, and it goes on in academic environments. Holding people accountable means to give grades for work actually done. You recognize the difference in quality. The faculty, in turn, are evaluated by their students. Being open to that kind of feedback allows for a level of confidence that what goes on in an academic environment will carry over into the future." (Malloy, 2007, p. 64)

SUMMARY

Sometimes teachers are called upon to rise above their personal needs for belonging. When standing on principle they do not always receive the approval of their colleagues. This occurs not only in the school setting but also at professional gatherings such as conventions. There principled educators face unique challenges.

Teachers have other opportunities to send the message of dignity and integrity. They do so by how they dress, how they respond to groups formed in buildings based on perceived status, how they model kindness and integrity, and how they respond to unethical behaviors of other staff members. Sometimes ethical educators use strategies to relate to these individuals, and other times they view them without judgment and also with humor. Collectively, various faculties combine and can contribute positively to the creation of ethical systems.

REFERENCES

Johns, B., McGrath, M., and Mathur, S. 2006. *Surviving internal politics within the school.* Lanham, MD: Rowman & Littlefield Education.

Malloy, E. B. 2007. Final thoughts: How does one become a person of character? *St. Thomas* XXIII(1): 64.

CHAPTER 11

Working with Parents

A group of teachers from Harris School like to go out together on Friday after school to a local restaurant for a quick cup of coffee to unwind before their weekends. They have always made a rule that they will not talk about their students but talk about their own families and interests. After a rough week at school, a new teacher to the group, Anna, suggests that they go to a local bar. Some of the teachers are reluctant to go but don't want to be spoilsports, so they agree except for Joni, who decides to pass. Joni doesn't like the idea of being seen in a bar in their small community.

The teachers who go to the bar learn quickly that Anna likes to drink and has had three beers in the period of a half hour. She begins talking about a student in her class and unloads to the group about the problems she is having with the student. Her colleagues are torn—they want to help her but at the same time don't like talking about students at their get-togethers. A few of them wish they had stayed behind as Joni did. Betsy doesn't like what is going on so excuses herself, saying she needs to go home. The rest of the teachers, however, make the decision to go along with Anna. They ask her why she thinks the child is having problems.

At four beers, Anna goes on about how the child's parents are the problem. As she talks further, she gives background information about the parents. The other teachers finally recognize that this has gone too far and suggest they leave. Unfortunately, that decision was made too late. It seems that the couple who were sitting at the table behind the teachers had heard a great deal of the conversation and were the aunt and uncle of the student.

On Monday afternoon, the building administrator calls several teachers individually into his office and explains that he is investigating a complaint that has been filed with the superintendent and the school board by the student's parents.

Unfortunately, Anna spoke negatively about the parents and violated confidentiality by doing so with fellow teachers who did not really have the right to know all of the information they were provided; none of them came into contact with this student. Anna also talked publicly about a child and his parents where members of the public could hear. Anna may have been frustrated with the behavior of the student, but she had no right to unload her opinions on others publicly. She showed disrespect to the parents and violated confidentiality.

Anna was not acting in an ethical manner. Joni believed that the trip to the bar was not a good idea and used her good judgment not to go. Betsy went, but when she began to see what was happening she left; however, Betsy was called into the office for questioning because she had been associated with the group and seen in the bar.

RESPECTING THE NEEDS OF PARENTS

It is very easy for educators to criticize parents—after all, they don't know the struggles a parent is facing, and they don't live with the child. Anna was quick to blame the parents. Educators work with the children they serve for not even one third of a day; they don't have to deal with the child in the evenings or on the weekends when the parents might be tired or might have other priorities.

All of us may have become frustrated because the parent is not consistent in reading to the child or helping the child with homework; then we learn that the parent has a new baby at home; or we learn that the parent is holding down two jobs in order to pay bills. Before we ever criticize a parent, we owe it to that parent to investigate his or her needs. We work in today's schools with single working mothers or fathers who are trying their best to raise their children. Granted, parents may make mistakes and do, but we will not be as quick to criticize them if we understand their needs.

RESPECTING THE STRENGTHS AND WEAKNESSES OF PARENTS

Just as the work we do with students should be based on their strengths, so should our work with parents. We should look for the positive attributes of the parents as we work with them. We can establish a good working relationship with parents by utilizing those strengths. If parents get their children to school on time and every day, we should recognize that. If parents always respond to our notes, we should thank them.

When we give homework, we need to think of the effect that homework will have on the family. Can the parent help the child with this specific homework assignment? Will the homework result in three hours of hassles for the family because it is difficult for the student?

Sometimes we get so frustrated with what the parents do or don't do that we become very negative toward them and don't stop to reflect on their strengths and build on those strengths. Instead we focus on their weaknesses and fail to recognize that they may be doing as well as they can do. Most parents want the best for their child; some may not know how to achieve that. Ethical educators set the student and the family up for success, not failure.

REMAINING PROFESSIONAL WHEN WORKING WITH PARENTS

One of the authors remembers an incident where a parent came into the school where the author was the administrator. The parent was very upset because the student didn't get to eat all of his lunch. The reason the student didn't get to eat his lunch was that he yelled out, "I hate this slop!" and proceeded to throw his lunch at the teacher. The student obviously could not eat the rest of his lunch.

The parent came into the school and started screaming at the administrator: "You have to give him his lunch; he has a right to his free lunch." The administrator was very upset by the comment. She had tried to give the student his lunch, but the student had chosen to throw it. However, she had to maintain both her internal and external control and explain to the parent very calmly that the student had been provided his lunch, and he had made the choice to throw it at the teacher.

As the author is writing this, there is a news story where a parent is angry and proceeds to throw grapes at the school board members at a school board meeting. This type of behavior is obviously very disruptive and not acceptable. Police were called to remove the parent from the meeting. It would have been very easy for a school board member to "lose her temper" and become defensive and yell at the parent. However, when a parent does not act appropriately, a school board member is not justified in behaving inappropriately and unprofessionally.

The educator must always remember that it is his or her responsibility to remain professional. There may be times when a parent will swear at you or call you names. The parent may call you on the telephone and cuss you out. The question is, "How much of this behavior do you have to tolerate?" You certainly do not have to let the parent swear at you—if you do so, you are sending a message that it is okay to behave toward you in this manner. That is not a message you want to convey. When the parent engages in such behavior, calmly state, "I cannot talk with you when you are talking like that. When you are calm, we can continue a discussion." Then you should step away from the parent to convey the body language that you will not tolerate such language.

On the telephone, if the parent calls and is swearing, you should make a calm statement: "I cannot talk to you when you are swearing. I will need to hang up if you continue that language." You have provided a notice to the parent that you will not accept such treatment and will close the conversation.

If we are nice and treat the parent with respect, the parent will usually respect us. Picture this situation. Mrs. Krell has to come to the school to pick up her son, who is sick. Mrs. Krell is very angry when she arrives because she has a lot of errands to run and is upset that her child's illness will put her behind. She can't understand why the school just can't keep the student there. She comes in the door and reports to the office. The school secretary sees her and immediately says with a smile: "Oh, Mrs. Krell, we really appreciate your coming to get Justin—I know you have a lot to do, but we know we can count on you." With this verbal statement, the secretary defused a great deal of anger from Mrs. Krell. The secretary praised the parent for coming in, showed empathy, and set high expectations for Mrs. Krell.

There may be parents who cause you to feel fear. They may have a history of violence or may have threatened you in the past. In those instances, it is important that you not place yourself in a position where you are alone with the parent. If you believe that you might be in danger, you should alert your administrator and seek assistance. In these cases, it is always advisable to have witnesses. You may also sense that the parent might act inappropriately with you. You must set clear expectations for the parent that you will not tolerate such behavior and are going to find help.

Just as we are a role model for students, we must also be a role model for the parent on how to deal with situations calmly and professionally.

HANDLING CONFIDENTIALITY ISSUES

In the example of Anna, she certainly violated confidentiality laws. She was sharing information about the student and the parents with fellow teachers who did not need to know the information. She also shared the information in a public place where individuals overheard what was said.

Confidentiality with Parents

A common phenomenon occurs when one student has gotten into trouble with another student. One parent comes in to the school and is very upset and wants to know what happened to the student who pushed his child. The teacher must be very careful to not disclose information about the other child; to do so violates that student's right to privacy. The teacher can provide general information about the event but must not get into providing information about the other student.

A situation might also occur when a parent wants to talk to one educator about another educator. When parents speak with a homeroom or classroom teacher or a special educator with whom they confide, they may express their sentiments about other staff persons. Perhaps they think the physical education teacher is too demanding on their child or the music teacher embarrasses their son when asking the child to match a pitch. The parents might speak to Casey's social studies teacher about their frustration with his math teacher or talk to the English teacher about the poor grammar of the new teacher from another part of the country. Maybe the parent of a student receiving special services will express to a special education teacher a preference for Robert's classroom teacher for the following term or ask a resource teacher how to avoid Melissa's being placed in Mrs. Smith's language arts class.

If a parent presents this information to a teacher, it is important for the teacher not to engage in discussion of personal qualities or other details about a coworker. It is not only unprofessional but also disloyal and can create ill will among staff members. A teacher presented with such information would be wise to suggest that the parent talk directly with the teacher of concern or bring the issue to a supervisory staff person. Relative to placements, special educators should note that they have no say in such matters if they do not. If they do have input, they can reassure the parent that they look at the big picture and place a student according to the team's view as to what is best at the time.

Confidentiality with Other Relatives

Children obviously have extended families, and sometimes children live with a relative other than the natural parent. When the teacher reviews his or her class roster at the beginning of the school year, the teacher must check with the principal to see whether there are any different living arrangements involved with any of the students. The teacher must learn from the building principal who is the legal guardian for the student, who is the custodial versus noncustodial parent, and whether there are any divorce decrees that prohibit the release of information to a parent. FERPA (the Family Educational Rights and Privacy Act) governs the release of information. States may also have an additional set of regulations governing how information is released. The building principal will have that information. It is important that information be released only to the legal guardian of the child.

Grandma might call about the child, and the educator is tempted to share a great deal of information about how the child is doing. If Grandma is not the legal guardian of the child, Grandma does not have the right to that information. Billy's aunt may stop you in the grocery story and ask how Billy is doing. First of all, it is not appropriate to discuss a child in the grocery store—there are many people who may pass by and hear the information. Tempted as you might be to discuss Billy's progress with his aunt, this is inappropriate. You are violating Billy's right to privacy because his aunt does not need to know the information.

Confidentiality with Other Agencies

The Family Educational Rights and Privacy Act (FERPA) outlines the releases that are needed by either the legal guardians or the child for school personnel to talk with other agencies. School personnel may share information with other public school personnel who have a need to know that particular information.

There are exceptions to the release of information. When there is a life-threatening situation, educators have the right to provide information to a mental health agency or a hospital. If a student is suicidal, the educator seeks the assistance of the building administrator and the social worker or counselor, and together they have the right to make a referral to a mental health agency. If the child faces a medical emergency, school personnel certainly must notify the parent right away but could release information that was needed to save the child's life.

Working with Foster Families and Surrogate Parents

In the reality of today's society, some children have been removed from their natural parents and been placed in foster care. Those children also have an assigned caseworker. Each state has specific laws that govern communication with foster families and the caseworker. It is important that educators work with their administrators to become very aware of these laws and regulations. It is very possible that the educator may have some contact with the child's biological parents, who may try to gain information about the child's progress. In those cases, the educator must work closely with the caseworker and the building administrator to determine how to deal with the particular situation.

In special education, there are provisions in the Individuals with Disabilities Education Act (IDEA 2004) that require the appointment of a surrogate for children who do not have a parent who can represent them. Surrogates are appointed and have the rights of a parent in special education issues—giving consent for case study evaluation and

placement in special education and participating in the IEP conferences. They also have the right to review the special education records
for the child. That surrogate may or may not be the foster parent, so it
is important that the educator know who the surrogate is. The administrator of the school will have that information. In this case, it becomes
confusing about what information can be shared with the surrogate versus the foster parent, but special education rights are given to the surrogate.

Home Visits

There was a time when teachers conducted many more home visits
than they do today. The challenges of our society have made us much
more cautious now. We may be placed in a very awkward position
walking into a home because we are not sure what we will find there.
We may find a parent alone and feel threatened by the situation. It is
unfortunate that we must be so careful nowadays because we can gain
a great deal of valuable information about the child's challenges and
culture by going into the home. Home visits should certainly be maintained, but educators should not go alone. It is appropriate to go with
another educator, perhaps the school social worker or the school counselor or the school administrator.

Phone Behavior

Extreme caution is needed when dealing with individuals over the
telephone. Someone may call and identify himself as the parent of the
student but in fact may not be that individual. When an educator receives a call from an individual and is not sure that the person is who
he says he is, the educator should ask for the individual's phone number and state that he will call the individual back. This gives the educator the opportunity to seek further information and to verify that the
individual is who he says he is.

Caution must be taken when speaking on the telephone to assure that
the phone conversation is not being overheard by another individual.
Cell phones are wonderful tools to assure better communication but
have a large drawback—people have become very careless about talk-

ing on cell phones in public places. The educator decides to return a call from a parent while she is at the printer or at a conference; someone else hears the conversation and receives information that he should not receive.

More schools have provided telephones in teachers' classrooms as a convenient mechanism for communication with parents. However, it is not appropriate to take a call when the children are in the classroom and can hear the conversation. Educators sometimes have the mistaken notion that the child doesn't understand what is being said, but that is not a safe assumption. Educators must learn to be very cautious and take calls only when children are not in the classroom.

Electronic Means of Communication

With the increasing use of e-mail systems, educators may choose to communicate with the parent utilizing this system. This is certainly permissible, but one must be very careful about what he or she says to the parent via e-mail. It is not advisable to discuss sensitive issues about the child via e-mail. Remember also that it is easy for someone to misunderstand what may be communicated electronically.

As more individuals utilize e-mail, they are getting careless about the correct use of grammar and spelling and are not writing in complete sentences. This can be very problematic because the parent can misunderstand what is being said. The parent may also be very offended that the educator did not use proper grammar and punctuation.

Many educators carry their laptops or PDAs with them everywhere they go. They want to always be electronically connected, and nowadays, with wireless communication, that is easy. This habit is certainly admirable, but individuals have to be very careful about where they are using their equipment. Is someone looking over the educator's shoulder and seeing what is being written to the parent? The educator may be keeping an electronic log about a student and decides to work on the log in the evening at the local wireless coffee shop. The educator may be so engrossed in her work that she doesn't notice that the person sitting behind her can see what she is typing. An educator may take his laptop or PDA with him to a ball game and decide to respond to his e-mails. He has received an e-mail from a parent, and the person behind him can see the response. Educators must always think ahead and be careful where and how they are communicating.

Communicating with Colleagues within the School about a Particular Student and His or Her Parents

Educators should remember that they should not be sharing information about a student or a student's parents with anyone who does not need to know the information. It certainly is important for the bus driver to know that Mrs. Jones, Jennifer's mother, has a concern about Jennifer's safety on the bus. However, it is not a concern to the bus driver that Jennifer's father and mother adopted Jennifer. It is certainly a concern to the cafeteria worker, bus driver, and substitute that Jennifer has a specific food allergy, but again those individuals do not need to know about the adoption. The fifth-grade teacher does not need to know that Billy, who is a first grader, has behavior problems that may be related to the fact that his father is an alcoholic. Educators should not share information with anyone unless they are able to give an affirmative answer to this question: "Does this individual need to know this information in order to interact with this student?"

A recent event occurred in a local school where teachers were sending e-mails back and forth about a student. A parent who was a computer whiz figured out how to access the school's e-mail system and gathered confidential information about students. This incident serves as a word of caution when communicating very specific information about students and their parents.

COMPASSIONATE HONESTY

We have a moral obligation to be honest with parents about the progress or lack of progress of their children. Failure to do so is not fair to the parent and paints an unrealistic picture of the child. It might also result in the parent's establishing too high or too low expectations. However, we also have the obligation to communicate the levels and needs of the child with compassion. Some educators do not want to tell the parent that his child is not progressing within the classroom; however, failure to do so is not fair to the parent.

One of the authors remembers attending many IEP meetings for students with disabilities. Classroom teachers did not want to discourage the parent and did not want to share the problems that the student was having in front of a number of other people. That was not fair to the parent and frankly was not fair to the other IEP team members who were trying to determine a placement based on the individual needs of the child. Information about the lack of skills or the behavioral problems of the student should be specific and not reflect exaggerations or opinions based on subjective information. An IEP meeting may be occurring because of the student's behavior problems. The teacher does not want to say anything negative so does not report important information (Johnny tried to choke another student; Sally spit in Billy's face).

Generally the rule of thumb should be to utilize the sandwich theory. Couch the inside of the sandwich (the concerns about the student that may be perceived as negative) with the positives.

It is particularly difficult to utilize the sandwich theory when referring to children with behavioral problems. The reality is that the teacher may be at his or her wit's end and says there is nothing nice that can be said about the child. Yet if we remember the importance of building on the strengths of the child, we can begin with strengths of the child, talk in specific objective terms about the concerns we have, and then talk again about what strengths are exhibited. It is always so important to close with the statement "I want us to work together to help your child."

WORKING AS A TEAM

The message to the parents should always be that we want to work together with them to help their child. Rather than pointing our fingers at the problems that a parent has and pointing out the parent's deficiencies, we want to communicate that we are there to work together to assist the child. When presenting a problem situation to the parent, we should approach it as a team effort ("How can we work together to improve Jesse's reading skills?").

REMEMBERING YOUR ROLE—RESPECTING BOUNDARIES

Becoming Friends with Parents after Their Child Comes into Your Class

We may meet a parent of one of our students and really "click" with that individual and want to become friends with the parent. We must proceed very cautiously in these instances because we may find ourselves playing favorites with the student or, through our friendship, begin confiding with the parent about problems with students within the classroom. This is not appropriate.

There are also parents who consciously work to create a friendship with the teacher so that they can find out the "real story" about what is happening in the classroom, and they believe that their child will have an advantage if they are friends with the child's teacher.

Becoming Friends with Parents Who Are Volunteers

Sometimes educators become well acquainted and familiar with parents who spend a lot of time volunteering at the school. Teachers become close with parents of students that they have taught, especially if they have taught siblings.

It may happen that due to the comfort level that teachers and parents have achieved with one another that the teacher feels relaxed in the presence of the parents, so much so that he begins to confide with the parents about classroom challenges. Descriptions of difficult students, even without using names, indicate to parents who these problem students might be.

Parents talk, too. The parent that the teacher takes into his confidence may then go to another parent, and together they can put two and two together and find out more than they should know. They may put the information together incorrectly and speak about a student in error.

Teachers need to be clear on their boundaries with parents. Though a parent may be someone that could be a potential friend, teachers have to continually remember that they are professionals and must keep the line clear between themselves and parents.

Having Children of Your Friends in Your Class

There will be times when you will have the child of one or more of your friends in your classroom. You are in a precarious position—one that requires you to exercise professional judgment and caution. You must draw the line between your friendship and your work as an educator. You will not be able to confide with your friend about what is happening in your classroom with specific students other than your friend's child. You will also need to monitor your own behavior in your relationship with the child, making sure that you are not playing favorites with the child because of your friendship with his parent.

Dating a Parent

On occasion, a single teacher will have a conference with a single parent of a student. During these exchanges, much confidential information is shared by the parent to a teacher. A teacher could have formed a close relationship with a student and fantasize about being married to the child's parent and being the mom or dad to this student.

Some organizations have policies about professionals dating clients. It is not often that you hear of a pediatrician or child psychologist dating the parent of one of the young people included in therapy or treatment.

Before allowing such fantasies to get out of hand, teachers need to know the district policies and conduct themselves professionally with all parents of their students. Certainly it would be out of bounds to start a personal relationship and be overly "understanding" to a parent in a difficult marriage or going through a divorce. Being empathetic and supportive is fine, but a teacher's primary goal is the education of the students in her classroom.

Educators, not Counselors

Some parents may become dependent on us for advice and support. While we can be a good listener and should be empathetic with the parent, we have to remember that we are not counselors. We have to be astute and look for signs that the parent may be utilizing us as a counselor and not a teacher. If we see the warning signs of this—asking for advice on personal issues that do not relate to the child's educational program or spending too much time with us—we then need to take a step back and let the parent know compassionately that we cannot play that role with them.

The Parent Who Is Overfocused

Sometimes parents become overfocused on their child, a certain aspect of your classroom routine, or a particular feature of your teaching style. They become too involved with the school situation and drop by unexpectedly much too often. When this occurs, the educator must have a strategy in place so that he does not have to continuously engage in unproductive exchanges with this parent. Perhaps other staff could be alerted to come to your room or phone you when they see the parent coming. The parent could then be diverted to another activity.

FORMING OUR OWN OPINION

The teachers lounge or faculty meetings can be hotbeds for gossip about students and their families. How many times have we heard the previous teacher of the student say, "Marcy's mother is a pain in the butt. She will drive you up the wall." We then have developed a preconceived notion about Marcy's mother and may avoid her in any way we can. We have based our opinion on another individual's opinion and have changed our behavior negatively in doing so. When we hear the opinions of others, we owe it to the parent whom we have not met to not judge them until we have met and worked with them and formed our own impressions.

SUMMARY

Exercising ethical behavior when working with parents requires us to treat parents with respect, recognizing their needs, strengths, and weaknesses. We must establish a professional relationship with them that exemplifies a positive attitude that we want to work together with them as a "team."

CHAPTER 12

Behavior Management

Mr. Black, a teacher's aide, is responsible for monitoring the behavior of eight students in a special education classroom during the lunch period. Jeremy, a nine-year-old, is joking with the other children—Mr. Black loudly tells him to stop. Jeremy starts arguing with Mr. Black. Mr. Black announces in front of all the students in the lunchroom: "Jeremy, you're getting on my nerves—quit acting like a baby."

Jeremy argues that he is not a baby. Mr. Black announces: "I am tired of your garbage. You are going to time-out." Jeremy says: "You can't make me." Mr. Black says: "Oh yes I can, watch me." Mr. Black then grabs Jeremy, picks him up, and carries him to the time-out room. Jeremy is fighting with him all the way to time-out. When they get to time-out, Mr. Black restrains Jeremy by putting him on the floor facedown. Jeremy continues to struggle.

The teacher, Mrs. Benson, is sitting in the lounge, and another teacher comes in and tells her what is happening. Mrs. Benson is irritated that her lunchtime has been disturbed but decides to go out and see about the problem. She goes by the time-out room and sees Mr. Black restraining Jeremy alone. She decides that there is no need for her to assist and goes back in the lounge to finish her lunch.

When Jeremy goes home he has bruises on him. His parents file a report with the Department of Children and Family Services and the police department. There is an investigation that occurs.

Mr. Black eventually loses his job over the situation. He was not supposed to restrain a student alone and did so. In fact, there were bruises on Jeremy, and Mr. Black had failed to follow the school's procedures; he was not to restrain a child alone.

It was apparent that Mr. Black did not act ethically in his behavior toward the student and made many errors—public embarrassment of the student, getting into a power struggle with the student, restraining the child alone, and utilizing a very restrictive restraint.

However, the teacher also failed to act professionally and ethically. Mrs. Benson was responsible for the supervision of the aide and failed in her job to supervise the individual. She knew of the situation and ignored it. In her eyes she did nothing wrong, but she certainly did. The teacher failed to meet her professional responsibility.

This chapter deals with the complexities of assuring that we are ethical when incorporating behavioral interventions in our classrooms and schools. With the increasing population of students with behavioral problems coming into our schools, it is critical that we maintain order and a positive school climate through an ethical approach to behavioral interventions.

Monitoring our own ethical behavior in teaching students with behavioral problems can be a challenge; at times the behavior of the students may bring out the worst in us, and we may find ourselves engaging in inappropriate behaviors as a result of the student's "pushing our buttons." It is critical that we continually evaluate our behavioral interventions to assure that we are being fair to our students.

PROTECTING THE PHYSICAL, MENTAL, AND EMOTIONAL WELL-BEING OF THE STUDENT

We often hear the phrase "First do no harm." This certainly applies when we are working to improve the positive behavior of students. However, how do we determine whether a behavioral intervention we have used has harmed a child? We may not have physically harmed the child, but we may have harmed the child emotionally by the words we have used. To help educators to determine the appropriate verbal and nonverbal techniques that should be used, these authors recommend the strategy "build the student."

As we discuss in this chapter, the educator must always ask herself whether the behavioral interventions utilized do no harm; the goal is building students up. Ethical educators do no physical, mental, or emotional harm to students. With that in mind, we start this chapter with the critical component of behavioral interventions—respectful treatment of students.

RESPECTFUL TREATMENT OF STUDENTS

Many children are coming into today's schools and classrooms fragile and vulnerable. Our words can be the impetus for them to have a positive experience and to be able to cope with the tragedies that they have had to face. Our words can also be the impetus for a negative school experience and may add another crushing blow to their already weakened tolerance for all of life's challenges. Our words therefore must be utilized very carefully and must be designed to build on the student's strengths.

One of the authors remembers well the college teacher that she had for an arts methods class. The author was to create a papier-mâché product. Not having a great deal of artistic talent, the author worked very hard on the project and was pleased with the final product that she had spent many hours creating. When she arrived in class, the teacher went around to each student, viewing the papier-mâché product that each had created and making comments in front of all the students. To some students she would make positive comments, and they would beam. To some students she made negative comments, causing them to bow their heads in embarrassment. When she arrived at the author's desk, the author was sure she would receive a positive comment. Instead, the instructor took one look at the papier-mâché product and said, "That's trite."

The author felt crushed—after all, she had worked hard on the project and had put forth her best effort. She also felt very embarrassed in front of the other students. While hopefully today teachers have learned it is not a good idea to embarrass students in front of peers, this teacher did just that. She made a lasting impression on the author—the author hates art to this day. However, a positive outcome occurred. The author determined that she would not engage in such behavior with any students with whom she worked. That one word "trite" was not respectful and served to destroy any love of doing art. The ethical educator chooses words carefully and does not utilize words that are destructive in nature and certainly does not embarrass a student in front of peers.

Educators are occasionally caught yelling at students—a technique designed to intimidate students. Such bullying and intimidation techniques are inappropriate for the school/classroom. Educators are misusing their power over the students.

Words can be harmful to students—making lifelong impressions on them that may change the way they perceive a certain subject. The teacher must choose words carefully. The educator's job is to build students, not destroy their attitudes about a given topic.

ETHICS IN BEHAVIOR MANAGEMENT GOES FAR BEYOND WHAT IS LEGAL

Many states have specific legislation that governs the use of behavioral interventions—some states have very specific laws and regulations that govern the use of time-outs and physical restraint. Some states prohibit the use of corporal punishment within the schools. It is critical that all educators have a thorough understanding of what is allowed and prohibited within the state. If the school district in which they are employed does not provide the information and the training for that, it is the obligation of the teachers to learn what laws and regulations exist and what those laws and regulations say. Resources to learn more information are available through professional organizations, state government websites, and policy manuals within the school district.

Educators must learn their legal responsibility and take that responsibility seriously. However, ethics in behavior management goes far beyond what is legal. The legal parameters are a starting point, but beyond those legal responsibilities, the educator must be cognizant of management techniques that are respectful and ethical. Mrs. Benson, the teacher who chose not to become involved in the situation involving her student and the aide in her classroom, did not commit an illegal act but certainly behaved unethically.

As another example, some states allow corporal punishment within the schools. Yet, we are role models for our students. How can we as educators hit students and tell them that they cannot hit other people? If we are teaching by example, we must set a positive one.

Many states allow the use of physical restraint when a student is harming him- or herself or others. School personnel should be trained in appropriate physical restraint techniques and should receive refresher classes. However, an educator could be following the letter of the law and utilizing the physical restraint techniques that are legally permissible, but the educator may not be acting ethically when he is involved in a restraint with other team members and puts unnecessary pressure on the student.

Some states provide guidance in the appropriate use of time-outs, and the educator may follow the wording in the law; yet the teacher is irritated with the student and decides to leave the child in time-out longer than was outlined in the school's policy because she is upset with the student. Time-out is allowed under state law where this teacher lives, but the teacher is misusing it.

MONITORING OUR OWN BEHAVIOR

Because the behavior of students impacts our behavior and our behavior impacts students, we must continually monitor what we are doing that may be resulting in specific undesirable behaviors. We may be, and often are, the antecedents or trigger for a particular behavior. While none of us wants to think that we "set up" students, sometimes we do. We know that when we raise our voice with a student that it will agitate the student and result in behavior problems. We know that when we give the student work that is too difficult for him to do independently that the student is likely to rip up the paper. These authors have heard teachers say that they just wanted to get the student out of their classroom, and they did something that would result in the student's being sent to the office.

Picture this scenario: Mrs. Stallings is having difficulty with a student, and the principal tells her she cannot refer him until she has documented at least 10 incidents of "aggressive behavior." She thinks the child should be referred, so she places the student in a situation where she knows he will act up. Granted, she is frustrated with the questionable system that the principal has created, but she engaged in inappropriate behavior.

The teacher may respond inappropriately to a specific behavior that a student exhibits. The student learns how to "press the teacher's buttons." The student has learned that if he calls the teacher "fatty," the teacher will become upset and send the child to the office. Granted, name-calling is bothersome to all of us, but we need to be able to deal with the behavior in an appropriate manner. If the student thinks the teacher is bothered, the student will continue to engage in the behavior, and the teacher finds himself sending the child to the office more and more. Excluding the child from the classroom repeatedly causes many students to fall further behind in class.

The ethical teacher constantly asks herself whether the behavior exhibited by the student is brought about by the teacher's actions or whether the behavior the student exhibits results in the teacher's using inappropriate behavior-management techniques. If the teacher is frustrated with the actions of the student, she should seek out assistance from specialists or should engage in additional professional development to learn new tools for behavioral interventions.

MAINTAINING OUR INTEGRITY THROUGH MAINTAINING THE INTEGRITY OF SPECIFIC BEHAVIORAL INTERVENTIONS

Oftentimes the educator may try a specific behavioral intervention with a student for a period of time. When questioned about the effectiveness of the intervention, the educator complains, "It just didn't work." It may not have worked because the intervention was not used as it was intended. With the increasing body of research to show the effectiveness of positive behavioral interventions and the body of knowledge that exists that shows how a specific consequential intervention should and should not be utilized, we owe it to our students to make sure that the interventions being implemented are being utilized the way they were intended.

As an example, the educator might establish a contract with a student. The educator establishes specific behaviors for the student to meet and then determines the consequences if the student does not engage in those specific behaviors. However, the correct use of a contract should focus on one or two behaviors, with a desired short-term reward/recognition for exhibiting those behaviors.

Time-out is one of the most frequently abused behavioral interventions. It can be extremely effective if used appropriately but can be very

ineffective if not used correctly. Time-out is an extinction procedure—
it is the contingent withdrawal of reinforcing stimuli thought to be
maintaining the inappropriate behavior (Johns and Carr, 2002). Time-
out should be very short in duration, and during the short duration of
time the student is ignored—not given any positive reinforcement.
Time-out is not effective if the educator, after the time-out, does not
positively reinforce the child when the child engages in appropriate behavior. Yet these authors have seen educators send children home and
call it time-out. Educators have also placed children in a hallway or in
the principal's office for extended durations of time. These strategies
are not the correct use of time-out.

Before utilizing any intervention, the educator must study the appropriate use of and the effectiveness of the intervention. We owe that to
the students we serve. Such websites as www.pbis.org have been designed to provide a wealth of information about the effectiveness of
specific interventions.

FULFILLING OUR RESPONSIBILITY—NOT TURNING THE OTHER WAY

Within a school, educators accept the responsibility to work as a team in
order to teach children appropriate behaviors. That responsibility is a serious one. When an educator sees a student who is not in his class engage
in an inappropriate behavior and the educator ignores that behavior by ra-
tionalizing to himself that "this child isn't my worry or responsibility,"
the educator is not fulfilling his role. Further, when the student is allowed
to engage in inappropriate behaviors and the student sees that nothing is
done, a negative message is conveyed to the student—it is okay to mis-
behave.

Educators walk a fine line between interfering with the behavioral
management of another teacher and fulfilling their responsibility to
teach children appropriate behavioral skills in the educational setting.
However, when a teacher sees a child engaging in a violation of the
school's rules, the educator has the responsibility to tell the student's
teacher so the teacher can intervene with the student.

When an educator observes a teacher engaging in an inappropriate
intervention with a student, he or she has a responsibility to report that
interaction to the building administrator—the educator is not tattling

but accepting the team responsibility of appropriate behavioral interventions for the students within that school.

In a recent case, the school custodian and a teacher observed a fellow teacher dragging a student down the hall by his hair. The school custodian and the other teacher discussed what they should do. The school custodian believed that the incident should be reported immediately to the school administrator. The other teacher was reluctant—she didn't want to lose the friendship of the teacher who engaged in the inappropriate intervention, and she was afraid of being ostracized by her peers. The custodian went to the administrator and reported the incident, and a thorough investigation occurred. The teacher received a formal reprimand for her behavior, and a report to the Department of Children and Family Services in the state yielded a founded report of abuse. The sad ending to this story is that the custodian who filed the original complaint was ostracized by other staff members who defended the actions of the teacher.

The custodian was acting ethically—taking her responsibility seriously. The teacher who dragged the student down the hall was not acting ethically, and the teacher who turned the other way and would not report the action was not acting ethically.

In a recent Ninth Circuit Court case in 2007 (*Preschooler II v. Clark County Sch. Bd. of Trustees*), school officials turned the other way when a special education teacher was allegedly physically abusing a four-year-old preschooler with a disability. The school officials tried to argue that they were immune from any action that might be taken against them. The court ruled that supervisors are responsible for the actions of their employees if they know an individual is violating a child's rights. The court stated that when school officials know or believe that a student is being abused, they must immediately report that abuse to appropriate authorities. Failure to do so can result in an official's being held personally liable for violations of a student's constitutional rights (Slater, 2007).

ESTABLISHING APPROPRIATE RELATIONSHIPS WITH STUDENTS

In an effort to help students who may be troubled, some educators will single students out and take them home with them or let students sleep on their couch at night. They believe that they can improve a student's behavior if they establish a more personal relationship with the student.

Educators must be very careful and separate their professional role from a personal role. Good educators want to assure that they help their students and establish a positive relationship with them. However, engaging in certain behaviors causes problems for a teacher. The teacher must remember her role and instead of meeting these needs for a roof over a student's head or a meal at her home, the teacher's role is to work with the administration to connect the student and her family with services that can be provided by other agencies.

When teachers allow students to come into their homes, especially a child alone, they are blurring the line between a professional and personal relationship that can become problematic. Imagine Mrs. Jones, a divorced mother of three, who wants to help a teenage boy and allows that boy to "crash" on her sofa. While the encounter may have been innocent on the part of Mrs. Jones, Mrs. Jones may be setting herself up for serious problems. In a true example, an educator allowed this to happen. It turned out that the student was engaged in illegal drug trafficking, and there was a warrant for his arrest. A colleague at the school reported the situation to the local police department, and the teacher was charged with aiding a criminal. Stories were rampant that she was having a relationship with the student.

We live in a changing society where all educators must be very cautious about bringing students into their homes. Imagine the teacher who decides to take six or seven of her students into her home. When the students leave, the teacher finds items that have been taken. The teacher is in a major dilemma—does she report this to the police and instigate an investigation of a crime?

Educators must show that they genuinely care about the students but must remember that they are in a professional role with their students—they can care for and meet the educational needs of a child without blurring the line of becoming too personal. Before an educator engages in any activity with a student, she must weigh the possible outcomes of that activity.

INAPPROPRIATE PHYSICAL INTERACTIONS

As seen in the case of Mr. Black, educators must use physical restraint only when a student is endangering self or others. Because of actual cases of deaths of children and adults when being physically restrained, staff should never utilize physical restraint unless they have been well trained on an ongoing basis. Staff should never restrain a child alone. Educators want to avoid any physical confrontation with a student— getting into a one-on-one battle with a student is very unproductive and inappropriate for an educator. Physical restraint is designed to hold a student with the least amount of pressure until the student is calmed down.

Any physical restraint must also consider the medical problems that the student may have. As an example, a student with asthma should not be placed in any restraint that could prevent adequate breathing.

Staff who are angry at a child at the time of a needed restraint should not be involved in the restraint—with their anger toward the child, staff may place undue physical pressure on the child. As has been discussed previously, staff must monitor their own behavior and their own feelings about the student. Detailed written records must be kept about any use of physical restraint. Females must be very cautious in the restraint of males, as should males restraining females. When students are being restrained frequently, then it is a signal to staff that this may not be an appropriate intervention, and the educator has a responsibility to bring a team of individuals back together to determine whether this is an appropriate intervention.

An increasing number of states have passed legislation governing the use of physical restraint. It is incumbent on all educators to know the laws in their states that govern the use of restraint and to not engage in such practices unless they have been trained and are part of a team.

AVERSIVE BEHAVIORAL INTERVENTIONS

There are a number of aversive behavioral interventions that are not prohibited by law or regulations, yet those behavioral interventions are not appropriate and are not ethical to use.

A recent report from a student teacher to one of the authors indicated that the student teacher observed the teacher blowing a whistle in a student's ears when the student misbehaved. This is an inappropriate aversive measure that is probably not prohibited in many state laws and regulations, but it is certainly inappropriate and abusive to a student.

Many years ago, the use of electric shock was used with children with autism when they were engaging in self-destructive behavior. Not too long ago, a case was reported where the use of shock was still being used in specific group homes.

Some educators utilize the removal of privileges, which is certainly appropriate in many cases. However, the removal of a right is not appropriate; neither is the excessive removal of a privilege. As an example, the teacher should not deny the child his lunch. Some schools do delay lunch for the student, which may be an effective intervention for some students for a short period of time, but the student should be given his lunch within a reasonable period of time that lunch would be served.

Some educators remove the student's physical education period. In most states, physical education is a mandated subject for students and should not be removed. Recess is a privilege for students, and some educators remove a child from recess for a period of time. Unfortunately, some educators remove the child from recess for the remainder of the year—this is ineffective for the student because once the teacher takes everything away from a student, there is nothing else to take away and the student has no reason to behave. Removal of recess should be for short periods of time—usually only for a few minutes.

EXCESSIVE REMOVALS THROUGH TIME-OUT OR SUSPENSION

Educators must adopt the philosophy that they are in their positions to educate students and keep them in school in order to do so. If educators are to be instructional leaders, their goal must be to ensure that students are at school in order to receive that education. Schools must work to assure that there is a whole array of placement options for students to meet the diverse needs of students with behavioral problems. School personnel may become frustrated with those diverse needs and because of that frustration begin to engage in exclusionary practices. Those exclusionary practices such as excessive use of time-outs or suspensions/expulsions result in the loss of instructional time for students and don't provide students with the skills to be able to cope with the school setting.

Certainly there are times when a student needs to be removed because of disruption or danger. In those instances, the removal should be done for a short period of time, and during that time the educators must investigate thoroughly whether a different educational setting is needed for the student.

To keep utilizing removal when it is ineffective and when it is excessive is not in the best interest of the student. The removal may give the educator immediate relief from the stresses of the student, but it is not helping the student. Furthermore, it is causing the student to get further behind in school. The student is being "pushed out of the educational system." Unfortunately, when that occurs the student may be pushed into the juvenile justice system. Suspension is an ineffective behavioral intervention, yet it continues to be used in the schools. In one state, the number of students suspended from school in 2002–2003 reached its highest level in a decade—a 9.9 percent jump from the previous year (Johns and Carr, 2007; Archer, 2003).

One of the authors recently received an e-mail from a colleague saying that school personnel in the system in which she worked had reviewed the language in the Individuals with Disabilities Education Act of 2004 (IDEA 2004) and decided that they could keep suspending students with disabilities for 10 days at a time on numerous occasions. This was a gross misinterpretation of the law. However, beyond that it was a very sad commentary on the mind-set of some educators—how can we get around the system and repeatedly remove students from school?

When interventions such as time-out or suspension are repeatedly being used with students, educators have an ethical responsibility to come together as a team and to look at more appropriate interventions and placement for the students.

GUIDANCE FOR THE ETHICAL USE OF BEHAVIORAL INTERVENTIONS—QUESTIONS TO ASK ONESELF

When assuring that we are utilizing behavioral interventions that are ethical for students, we must ask ourselves these questions:

Would I want myself or my child treated the way I am treating this child? Before we utilize any behavioral intervention with a student, we should ask ourselves this question. In the case of the teacher who told the author her work was trite, if she had asked herself that question, she may have chosen a more constructive comment designed to assist the author.

Would I utilize this behavioral intervention if there were an observer in the room or if I were being videotaped or audiotaped? When we are working with children and engaging in interventions that can certainly have a profound impact on their lives, we need to stop and ask ourselves this question. We live in a day and age of accountability, and we should not be engaging in any behavioral interventions that we wouldn't want to be on tape.

Is the behavioral intervention based on the individual needs of the student? Ethical educators owe it to the children with whom they are entrusted to consider the individual needs of the child. A student may come into the classroom and put his head down on the desk. The teacher may decide to confront the student in front of the rest of the class. After all, she can't allow the student to sleep in her class. However, a quick flip through the morning's newspaper showed that his mother was arrested the night before. The needs of that child are critical. The teacher doesn't want the child to sleep in class.

The more appropriate intervention would be for the teacher to call for the social worker or the guidance counselor or the principal to come and get the student and spend some positive time with him.

In a true story about a young man with whom one of the authors worked, his individual needs had to be considered when planning behavioral interventions. Jamie is deaf and was adopted by a lovely family when he was about three years of age. Not a great deal was known about his natural family, but it was known that his parents had locked him in a dark closet for long periods of time when he misbehaved, and he had been very traumatized by the experience. At school it was quickly learned that he never wanted to be left alone. Because of his previous experience, it was determined that a time-out room should not be utilized as a behavioral intervention for him.

Have I investigated the nature of the student's behavioral problem that results in the need for a behavioral intervention? Behavior is communication, and when students are behaving in a certain manner, they are trying to tell us something, and we need to figure out what message the behavior is communicating to us. If we remember that some students engage in certain behaviors because of fear, it will help us to be understanding in the use of our interventions.

Let's take the example of Sammy. Sammy is in sixth grade and prides himself on being a leader—in fact on the street he is a leader in his gang. The teacher has the requirement that all students have to read in front of the class. Sammy reads at only a third-grade level. When he is asked to read, he starts yelling and provokes a confrontation with the teacher. He is afraid to read in front of the class. The teacher who knows this information and repeatedly puts that student in such an embarrassing predicament is not acting in a responsible, ethical manner.

A great deal of work has been done in the area of functional assessment—understanding the function of a specific behavior a student exhibits. Students may act out to get access to attention, to escape a particular task, or for a sensory reason—the room is too noisy, or the light is bothering the student. It is up to us to work with others to determine the function of the behavior and then to plan an intervention that is appropriate to meet the child's unmet need.

Is the behavioral intervention I have chosen to use appropriate for the developmental level of the student? One of the observations that these authors have made is that some of the behavioral interventions we utilize are not appropriate for the level of the student. It is not realistic to expect a kindergartner to sit in a chair for 40 minutes without the opportunity to move. One must be very careful that because a child is large for his age, we may expect more from him; yet socially and emotionally, that child may not be as mature as his size or even his age.

Have I included positive interventions in any plan to increase appropriate behavior? There is a large and consistent body of research that states that if we want to change behavior and gain resulting long-term changes in that behavior, we must utilize positive behavioral interventions—interventions designed to increase appropriate behavior. Students should receive consequences for inappropriate behaviors, but any plan must include recognition for the positive behavior in which the student engages.

We often just expect students to behave appropriately, and we take it for granted—saying to ourselves that they shouldn't be recognized for what they are supposed to do in the first place. However, all of us work for positive recognition for a job well done. Anytime we sit and collaborate on appropriate interventions for students, we must always assure that positive interventions are built into the plan.

Is the behavioral intervention I want to use based on scientifically based research and not on the latest fad? Too often, educators jump on bandwagons for the latest fads, which unfortunately appear often in education. In the area of academic and behavioral interventions, such fads run rampant. Someone is trying to "make a buck" and has a new magic cure for all of children's problems. False hopes are provided. Educators must work hard to assure that they are not being taken in by these fads. It is an educator's ethical responsibility to investigate any intervention that is being proposed for a student or the classroom.

Have I taught the student the appropriate behavior? We are often quick to criticize the child or her family for a specific pattern of behavior. We may also blame the child's parents for the child's behavior. It may be true that the child is engaging in a behavior that is acceptable in the home but is not acceptable within the school. Rather than criticizing the reality of the child's situation at home, we need to ask ourselves whether we have taught the child the appropriate behavior for school. We can no longer assume that children come to school knowing how to behave. We have to spend the time to teach them the behaviors that we expect, just as we teach academics. Our role is to teach—behavior and academics.

SUMMARY

When assuring that we are utilizing ethical behavioral interventions and making sure our own behavior is ethical, we must remember that our work is to teach and protect the children who are entrusted to our care. Any behavioral intervention should be designed to positively change the behavior of the student. Our goal should be to teach children the appropriate behaviors that we want them to exhibit and to reinforce them for engaging in those behaviors.

REFERENCES

Archer, J. 2003. Bay State sees big jump in student suspensions. *Education Week* 23(6): 19.

Johns, B., and Carr, V. 2002. *Techniques for managing verbally and physically aggressive students.* 2nd ed. Denver: Love Publishing.

Johns, B., and Carr, V. 2007. *Reduction of school violence: Alternatives to suspension.* Horsham, PA: LRP Publications.

Preschooler II v. Clark County Sch. Bd. of Trustees, 107 LRP 15146 (9th Cir. 2007).

Slater, A. 2007. Knowledge of teacher's abusive behavior forces officials to defend Section 1983 suit. *Special Ed Connection* (March 21).

CHAPTER 13

Maintaining Integrity across the Board

Susan and Cindy work in a middle school. Both are general education teachers. Susan teaches science, and Cindy is an English teacher. They are colleagues and work very well together; however, they are very much apart in their thinking and belief systems. Nothing appears to be similar between them. They seem to be at two opposite poles on many aspects of life.

Susan is involved in leadership activities and several clubs that promote the overall development and social competence of students. She spends time with her students, and they seem to trust Susan a lot.

Cindy teaches her classes and feels that she has done her job. She believes that she does not need to stick around after school to answer a few extra questions that her students or colleagues may have. She has given her seven hours, and she needs to go home and lead her life. She is a great instructor and teaches very well but does not offer any extra assistance to a student who may need it.

Susan, on the other hand, is sensitive to her students' needs. Recently, she was approached by a teenager, Heidi, on a Monday morning of finals week. Heidi asked Susan if she could wait after school to listen to her concerns. Susan had to take her dog to the vet's clinic at 5:00. She still felt the need to listen to her student who requested help. Heidi arrived at her office around 4:00 and asked if she had a few minutes. Susan said, "Sure," but she would have to leave within half an hour to get to her vet.

Heidi had a serious issue. Her mom was diagnosed with cancer. She was a great student and had missed a few assignments in the last couple of weeks due to the rough time at home. This was the finals week, and Su-san realized immediately that Heidi's concern was bigger than her pet's need for the doctor. She called her vet and rescheduled the visit. She called her home and asked her family to go ahead and not wait for her for dinner.

She asked her student, Heidi, if she would like to go for a cup of cof-fee and talk. She thought that Heidi needed to have a comforting envi-ronment.

They both went to a local coffee shop and spent an hour together. During this meeting, Susan found out that Heidi's mom has breast can-cer and would have to go through surgery the following week. Heidi would have to miss a couple days of school during this week and take her finals on Friday.

Heidi was very concerned about her mom as well as her own per-formance in class. She also worried about her future, which was unset-tled at this time. Susan assured her that she would talk to the counselor and let her know of this situation. She also said she would apprise all Heidi's teachers of her current situation and stay in touch with her dur-ing the week.

Susan went home with a heavy heart and spent some time with her family, her husband and her five-year-old daughter. She was relieved to see that they had had their dinner. She appreciated her husband for tak-ing care of the evening. Susan always felt fortunate about her support at home. She and her husband were very understanding of each others' needs. She stepped up to help out her husband when he needed to spend more time at work because one of his colleagues was going through some rough times. They have maintained mutual respect for each other's professional concerns.

The next morning, Susan went to the counselor's office and sought her advice on how to conduct Heidi's final exams in all subjects on Fri-day. The counselor created a schedule and advised all the related teachers. As a result, everyone assisted in this process. Susan also asked everyone to keep this information confidential. She kept checking with Heidi at home. Heidi informed her that her mother's surgery went fine and her mom would be back over the weekend. She added that her mother would have to go through chemotherapy and radiotherapy in the upcoming weeks.

Susan understood that she needed to be available to Heidi during this time, even if the summer was approaching. She knew that Heidi's needs may transpire during some odd hours or after-school hours. She wanted to offer Heidi her best possible support.

Educators move across groups and among organizational cultures. How does the educator maintain integrity at home, at work, in the community, and with personal relations? Where is the line in the impact one role plays on another role? This chapter defines integrity, discusses the characteristics of individuals with integrity, and discusses what type of life this individual leads.

The chapter also talks about how we can apply the principles of integrity in the various settings of our lives. It provides an explanation of some of the challenges that educators face in those settings. It may be easy for an individual to maintain integrity within one particular setting, but the same educator is challenged to maintain those standards in a different setting. Yet it is critical for the educator to maintain that integrity across the board—the individual must live these principles throughout all settings.

WHO IS THE EDUCATOR OF INTEGRITY?

Integrity is defined as the "quality or state of being of sound moral principle; uprightness, honesty, and sincerity" (*Webster's New World Dictionary of the American Language*, 1966, p. 759). The educator of integrity leads a life that is exemplified by honesty and uprightness. Those behaviors will become an ingrained part of the individual's existence.

One is reminded of the saying "Tell the truth the first time, and you don't have to remember what you said." When family members and colleagues know that they are able to rely on an individual to tell the truth and to be forthright with them, they can gain a sense of trust in that individual.

When a teacher says to another teacher, "Don't compromise your integrity," he usually means "act in correspondence with your own moral principles, and be consistent with your values." Do not get pressured by choices that are not beneficial for your students. For example, a teacher says to you that you do not have to teach some concepts in English because the study guide of the state test does not cover them, and students do not need to know them. Contrary to this advice, your moral principles state that the students need to master these concepts in order for them to understand more complex concepts. As an ethical educator, you need to adhere to your moral principles and stay diligent in your teaching.

CHARACTERISTICS OF EDUCATORS WITH INTEGRITY

Honesty

Compassionate honesty is practiced by the educator of integrity. While one should be counted on to be honest, one must provide the honest opinion with compassion. As an example, a fellow educator might ask the educator of integrity, "Do you think I am being too hard on my students?" The educator of integrity is torn; he knows that the colleague yells at her students and does not give students a chance to answer before she exclaims, "Well, you should have known the answer to the question." The educator of integrity might respond, "Do you think you give enough time to your students to answer your questions?" or "I know that sometimes it is hard to keep a calm voice with your students—I have to work on that."

We all might have been asked by a colleague, "Do you think I need to lose weight?" What a loaded question! An appropriate response, rather than saying, "Yes, you are overweight," might be "I think that we could all increase our exercise." Responding in a congenial and honest way, not necessarily in a brutal way, is another quality of an educator who has integrity.

Reliability

The educator with integrity knows that his students rely on him to be available at the time of need. If educators become inconsistent, unfair, and unreliable in their dealings, teaching will become chaotic. The classrooms will have no discipline. Teaching will be unpredictable, and students will feel lost.

If the teaching process is inconsistent, student performance may not reflect mastery of objectives to the extent to which the teacher originally envisioned and planned. The assessment may only demonstrate that the student excelled or failed in learning the aspect that is the subject of the exam. It may not demonstrate the level of inconsistency in the teaching process. But an ethical educator will be able to draw a conclusion that perhaps the poor performance is associated with her inconsistent teaching.

Reliability also depends on how consistently the teacher scores the assignments, applies behavior-management strategies, or maintains expectations for all students. For example, an educator is presented with four assignments that meet the requirements at the same level. However, the teacher gave these assignments four different grades, A, B, C, and D. Apparently, the teacher will be viewed as inconsistent in scoring. The student who got a D grade decides to draw her attention to this inconsistency; an unethical educator is likely to become defensive and will insist that faculty decisions are final. The ethical educator will address this issue of inconsistency and reflect on her scoring and correct it for all students. In addition, she will commit to working on being consistent in the future.

Another scenario is that a teacher, Heather, asks a question, and two students, Jamie and Mike, raise their hands to respond. Heather consistently picks Jamie to respond and inadvertently demonstrates bias against Mike. Mike begins to think that the teacher does not like him. One day he decides to approach Heather after school. Heather demonstrates integrity in her response and says, "Oh, I am sorry. I am glad you drew my attention to it. No, I really don't dislike you. I'll pay attention to my behavior."

Confidentiality

Integrity also means that the individual practices principles of confidentiality. When someone confides in the educator of integrity he or she knows that the information will go no further. In Heidi's case, she had complete trust in Susan. She knew that Susan would use sensitive information about her mom in a very careful manner.

Ethical educators are aware that they need to keep information confidential unless disclosure is required to prevent clear and imminent danger to a student. They consult with appropriate professionals when they are in doubt or when they have to make an exception. They are knowledgeable about the laws such as Family Educational Rights and Privacy Act (FERPA) that protect family and student rights.

Fairness

Fairness is defined as one's ability to make an educational experience equitable across students with various needs. An unfair educator provides unequal access to students in classes, plays favoritism, engages in private discussions regarding course materials with some students while excluding others, or provides them with more information than the rest of the students. A fair educator ensures that the learning process is equitable and that the special and diverse needs are met. Everyone, including those with special needs, should have the same level of opportunity to succeed.

This concept of fairness is extremely important when the teacher is dealing with students who have special needs or students who come from various cultural and linguistic backgrounds. The ethical educator is knowledgeable about their rights to an appropriate education and makes appropriate accommodations to meet their needs.

Mind-Set

Integrity is a habit of mind. The more the individual practices the qualities of integrity, the more those qualities become automatic and easier to follow. Integrity becomes a predictable pattern of life and an obvious trait across all situations in life.

Positive Attitude

The ethical educator has a positive attitude toward the profession. Oftentimes some educators who have been in the profession for too long develop a pervasive critical attitude toward life and forget why they are in this profession. They forget they need to cherish student growth and learning. They begin to criticize students, parents, systems, their colleagues, and administrators. At that point in their lives, they become unable to show integrity.

An ethical educator reflects on changes in his own thinking and keeps in mind positive approaches to managing behavior. He intervenes with a corrective intervention strategy in a nonpunitive fashion. He bases judgment on comprehensive and reliable data gathering. He is able to create a safe and nurturing environment that is conducive for student learning.

APPLYING PRINCIPLES OF INTEGRITY IN VARIOUS SETTINGS AND CHALLENGES FACED

As mentioned by Palmer (1997), "I am a teacher at heart, and there are moments in the classroom when I can hardly hold the joy. When my students and I discover uncharted territory to explore, when the pathway out of a thicket opens up before us, when our experience is illumined by the lightning-life of the mind—then teaching is the finest work I know." The process of teaching involves three strands: content, students, and teachers. The content is complex, as life and knowledge are oftentimes partial and flawed. The students we teach bring various levels of skills, diverse backgrounds, and a range of learning styles, and it becomes difficult sometimes to meet the needs of all students.

Finally, teachers who engage in teaching bring complexity in their own identities and various levels of integrity. It is the interaction of three strands that creates a teaching experience. The job of the teacher is to stay close to these strands.

PERSONAL LIFE AND ITS IMPACT ON THE EDUCATOR'S PROFESSIONAL ROLE

One cannot have one philosophy for personal life and another for work. They seem to intertwine and impact each other. Although much of integrity is based on one's upbringing and value system, it keeps developing as the inner core of the educator gets exposed to various situations. In other words, integrity is something that develops over time.

Ethical educators allow themselves to learn from their mistakes and constantly strive to refine their inner cores. They avail themselves of various professional development opportunities that focus on ethical decision making.

An educator's personal life affects her professional role. Every teacher brings her own moral self to interact in the process of teaching. Various system-related values associated with the teaching profession place role-specific constraints on teacher behavior and decision making. Although proper preparation and special concern for each student's success are essential for being an ethical educator, self-reflection is the key to developing integrity.

MAINTAINING INTEGRITY IN THE SCHOOL SETTING

The school consists of various environments—cafeteria, lounge, media room, library, meeting rooms—each requiring different behaviors from teachers. Some of these are more structured settings, such as the library and meeting rooms. One thing remains the same, and that is whether you demonstrate integrity in each of these settings. In the library, do you yourself follow the rules, even when students are not around? In more relaxed settings, do you begin to loosen up to the extent that you start sharing information that is confidential? In the cafeteria, do you leave your table clean after you have had your lunch? Are you a great listener in staff meetings? Are you viewed as a person who is trustworthy?

MAINTAINING INTEGRITY IN THE COMMUNITY

An ethical educator is one who identifies future trends and needs and develops systems for promoting positive changes and identifying problematic behavior ahead of time. If the educator has shoddy ethics, students can get away with little things, and then it catches on with other colleagues and plagues the whole community.

If you end up having a leader who lacks integrity, the whole community suffers, the leader loses credibility, and the whole school and the community are affected. Schools are built on community trust. Once a community loses trust in a principal, the school performance begins to go down. It is the same as violating personal trust. When a principal hides the results of the school performance or does not share the information in an accurate manner, it impacts the whole community. Parents feel cheated, and they lose faith in the educational system.

An ethical educator is an advocate for the public and has respect in the community. He is interested in community involvement and is able to use community resources to better serve his students. He believes that the purpose of education is to serve the communities of learners.

MAINTAINING INTEGRITY IN PROFESSIONAL ORGANIZATIONS

An ethical educator participates in educational professional organizations. She knows that they can have more influence over her profession and can do things that she individually cannot. The professional organizations work diligently to monitor and impact laws and regulations affecting educational practice.

In addition, professional associations provide educators an opportunity to interact with a group of peers. Ethical educators are also interested in advocacy and keep current on legislative, regulatory, and clinical practice issues that affect education. Many professional organizations, such as Council for Exceptional Children, are instrumental in setting teacher standards for education and have identified core competencies and critical behaviors that should be exhibited by educators.

SUMMARY

Teaching is a process guided by integrity. Effective teachers often think that their immediate obligation is toward the content that they need to teach. In addition, they focus on mastering effective teaching techniques. They also focus on student needs and make accommodations to meet their needs.

One should not forget about the integrity involved in the teaching process. Good teaching cannot be reduced to effective techniques or practices; the effectiveness comes from within, from the integrity of the teacher.

REFERENCES

Palmer, P. J. 1997. "The heart of a teacher: Identity and integrity in teaching." www.newhorizons.org/strategies/character/palmer.htm.
Webster's new world dictionary of the American language. 1966. Cleveland, OH: The World Publishing Company.

CHAPTER 14

A Call to Action

Kendra has worked in the middle school as an English teacher for the last 10 years. She prides herself in listening to all sides of a story and making her own decisions based on the information she can gather. Last year her building principal retired, and the assistant principal applied for the position. The assistant principal, Mr. Bates, was the favored choice of many of the staff members, but he did not get the position; instead, Grace Macauley from outside the district got the position.

Many of the staff members are very upset about Mrs. Macauley's getting the job. Over the summer, five of the teachers get together and discuss their plans to make the job very difficult for Mrs. Macauley. They plan to be very critical of her work and document any action that she takes that they don't like. This way, they can get rid of her and perhaps get the assistant principal the job he wanted in the first place. Mr. Bates is eager to be part of the plan to oust Mrs. Macauley and meets with the five teachers several times over the summer.

The five teachers who are heading the efforts call an informal meeting with all of the teachers in the building a few days before school starts and announce the plans to document anything that Mrs. Macauley does that any of the teachers don't like. Kendra attends the meeting to see what is happening. The five teachers announce the plans, and most of the other teachers agree with the plan; two seem to not agree, but they are afraid to speak up about their beliefs.

Kendra is very bothered by all of these actions that are taking place, even before the school year has started. Kendra believes that Mrs. Macauley should be given a chance to do her job. Kendra speaks up at

the meeting—she urges the teachers to give Mrs. Macauley a chance.
The other teachers frown at her comments and say she can do what she
wants, but they are going to work against the new principal.

A week before school starts, Kendra is working in her classroom, and
the new principal, Mrs. Macauley, drops by her classroom to meet her
and to see if there is anything she can do to help Kendra. Kendra says
that she is happy to meet her and looks forward to working with her
during the year.

Later that day, the assistant principal, Mr. Bates, comes by her room
and tells Kendra that he is disappointed to hear that Kendra does not
support him for the principal's position. Kendra explains to him that
she supports him in his current role and also supports Mrs. Macauley
in her new role.

Within the first week of school, the five teachers begin a petition to
request that the administration remove Mrs. Macauley from her posi-
tion. Even the few teachers who don't agree sign the petition. Kendra
refuses to sign the petition—she feels the new principal is being treated
unfairly and lets the teacher organizers know that she will not be part
of this effort.

How can we assure that we do our part to promote ethics—that we
don't buy into unfair treatment of others, complacency and apathy, going along with the crowd rather than taking a stand? Each of us has a
moral responsibility to do what we can to represent the educational profession in an ethical manner. Each of us has the responsibility to be a
leader in the educational field by our example everyday of the highest
ethical standards. Those standards should be ingrained within each of
us so that they are an integral part of our very existence. Ethics should
become a habit for each of us.

Kendra saw what was happening to Mrs. Macauley even before she
began the job. Kendra spoke up about the lack of fairness on the part of
the staff. She let Mrs. Macauley know that she wanted to work with
her; she treated her principal with respect and gave the principal the
chance to show her ability or lack of ability to do the job. She did not
jump to conclusions. She thought for herself. When the assistant principal talked to Kendra, Kendra answered that she wished to be fair to
both the principal and the assistant principal. She set a positive exam-

ple for all of the staff. She took a stand that, even though it made her very unpopular with the staff, was fair to the new principal.

MONITORING OUR OWN BEHAVIOR

Our call to action must be our commitment to continually monitor our own behavior to assure that we are engaging in the highest standards of ethics. What is happening in our society that causes some individuals to slip into "ethical lapses?" Individuals seek power and control and can get so wrapped up in that power and control that they begin to believe that they have the power to do whatever they want, even when what they want to do is not ethical. The five teachers in Kendra's building got carried away with the power they believed they had.

Picture this scenario: Mrs. Holden is elected the local teachers' union president. She is responsible for overseeing the actions of the administration to assure that the administrators are treating staff fairly. She oversees the finances of the union. She serves on the negotiating team for the district. She sees herself as a very powerful individual within her school building. She begins to believe that she is able to engage in a broad range of other activities because she is the union president.

She forgets that she was elected to represent the needs of her members; in meetings she begins representing her own personal needs at the expense of her members' needs. When other teachers ask her questions about her role, she becomes defensive and states that she is in charge. She misuses her position to get what she wants. She fails to frequently ask herself whether she is doing the job she was elected to do—representing the membership. She fails to monitor her own behavior.

Besides the need for power and control, individuals can become greedy and rationalize that their school district owes them more than they are given. Educators will begin to use school time for personal use or school property for personal use or the school's phone for personal use. They believe the school owes them this because they are not paid an adequate salary. They begin to justify what they are doing; after all, the school owes them. The more they have, the more they want—they become more and more greedy. We all know the stories of individuals who have enough money but want more and become obsessed with getting more.

We must monitor our behavior very closely to assure that we are not succumbing to behaviors that are characterized by control or greed. At the end of each day, we need to reflect on our actions of the day to assure that we are engaging in ethical behaviors. If we suspect that we are going down a slippery slope, we need to stop and change our behavior immediately. If we have done any harm to someone that day, we need to make it a point to treat that individual fairly the next day and in the future.

Avoiding a Negative Contagion

Integrity should be a way of life for each of us. It however becomes more difficult to maintain our integrity when everyone else is going in a different direction. Negativity can and often does become contagious, and it is hard not to "catch" it. It takes strength to recognize the negative contagion and to stand up with integrity and do the right thing. A helpful tip to remember when being faced with the beginning of a negative contagion within a group or at a meeting is to ask the group to look at all sides of the issue and to raise some questions that promote a thorough investigation of the situation.

Let's take the example of a group of teachers standing around and talking about the day they had at school. One teacher begins to talk about Mrs. Halton, the fifth-grade teacher, and how Mrs. Halton couldn't make Billy behave in the lunchroom. Another teacher chimes in and agrees and adds to the conversation: "I heard that she just can't control her class at all, and if she is smart she better start looking for another job." Another teacher chimes in and adds: "Well, I didn't want to say anything, but I saw Mrs. Halton's class the other day getting on the bus, and they were just terrible and she didn't do anything."

To avoid the negative contagion, another colleague states: "I wonder whether there is anything we could do to help Mrs. Halton? I have certainly had rough days and really appreciated it when one of you just listened to me at the end of one of those days. I think that tomorrow I will just ask her how she is doing and let her know I am here to listen if she needs a good ear."

Avoiding the Apathy Contagion

We all read the stories of someone being hurt and a crowd of people watching and not doing anything about it. Some educators may feel worn down and just give up. It takes too much of their energy to take a strong stand, so they just become apathetic and find themselves not standing for any principles. They just stay out of things through their apathy—they don't care. Their apathy is then interpreted as condoning inappropriate behavior on the part of their colleagues.

PROFESSIONALISM

True professional educators don't succumb to pressure, negativity, or apathy. When we see a breach of ethics in the news media or within our own immediate environments, we never allow those actions to cause us to think that perhaps we should loosen our standards. We should never allow ourselves to question our own ethics. Just because others are doing something wrong, it never gives us the excuse to engage in the same type of behavior. When others become catty, we should not think that we have a license to become catty. As part of professionalism, we should always ask ourselves, "Am I doing the right thing? Am I acting as a professional? What are the ramifications of my behavior? Am I a model for others?"

THINKING FOR YOURSELF

The path of least resistance is to believe one or more individuals and to go along with the crowd. Recently, one of the authors experienced a meeting where an officer wanted to remove someone from his position in the organization because of an action that the individual had taken. The individual was not present to defend himself. Some participants relied on the word of the officer. The author spoke up about the importance of giving the individual being accused a chance to tell his side of the story before making a decision.

It would have been easy to go along with the officer and some other members of the group and not think for oneself and fail to get the full story. When one accepts ethical standards and those become a habit, then it is easier for us to know that we must think for ourselves.

Maxwell (2003) reports that the more people that are involved, the greater is the pressure for conformity. This is true, especially when the leader of the organization, whether it is a teacher or an administrator, is putting pressure on the group to go along.

When this situation happened to the author in the example just given, she was reminded that the year before, in a similar meeting, someone had made an inaccurate comment about her when she was not present and able to defend herself. It reminded her about the golden rule: "Do unto others as you would have them do unto you." That rule must be at the forefront in our thinking when we are working with others.

BE AN INFORMED EDUCATOR

It is important for all educators to gather information that will help them make informed, fair, and ethical decisions. We must realize that there are at least two sides to any story, and we need to become informed so we can make those decisions. Too often, educators hear a presentation on a topic or are provided some information by a colleague; they don't research the topic themselves. Later they find out that they heard a skewed presentation or their colleague didn't have correct information; they then have made a decision based on erroneous information.

This author has had multiple experiences with individuals who take someone else's word about a printed document or a law; they fail to take the time to research the topic themselves. They later regret that they did not accept the responsibility for learning more about the topic.

Know the Laws

As we have discussed in earlier chapters, ethics goes way beyond doing what is legal, but knowing the legalities of situations and following the law is an important first step. It is critical that we know the laws that we are obliged to follow. It is not enough to take someone else's word about what a law or regulation states. One must learn the information firsthand. Laws and regulations are available to individuals via a variety of websites.

Verify Information Yourself

There are so many times that someone will make a statement that is not based on fact but is his or her own opinion. When a colleague says that another colleague is "just plain lazy and sits behind her desk all day long," we should recognize that such a comment is very subjective. We should ask that individual to clarify the information with a statement such as "Why do you say that?" or "What has happened that makes you say that?" This questions the subjective statement and also provides us with more information about the statement. We then must be very careful that we don't use that statement to bias our opinion of either individual—the one who made the statement and the one who is being discussed. We should collect information ourselves and make a decision based on factual information and our impressions of those individuals.

Another common practice is to discredit the individual who provides accurate information. Some will say that the person doesn't know what she is talking about or that person must have misunderstood the information. The ethical educator never discredits another individual; he gathers the information himself and lets the information speak for itself.

Ignorance Is No Excuse

How many times have we heard a colleague say, "I don't want to know about it." That may be a common response when an individual does not want to bias herself against an individual; but unfortunately it may be an individual's response when she does know what is happening in an unethical situation and she chooses to ignore it. When we ignore, we condone. When we ignore, inappropriate behavior escalates.

Never Prejudge Others

Mr. Cooney transfers to your school building as the third-grade teacher, and someone says, "I heard he was transferred because he likes to touch the female teachers." While that may naturally put you on guard about Mr. Cooney, you should not spread that gossip, and you should say to yourself that you will not prejudge Mr. Cooney but will give him a chance in your school. You will also want to listen for additional information about why Mr. Cooney left his former school.

RESPECT RATHER THAN RETALIATE

If we adhere to the premise "Do unto others as you would want them to do unto you," we will work to treat all individuals with respect. You may not agree with their actions, or you may have heard rumors about them; however, all individuals should be treated with respect. Unfortunately, many individuals adhere to the adage "Don't get mad, get even." We are upset with an individual because of a particular behavior, and we decide to retaliate against that individual. We tend to hold grudges and may become obsessed with how we can get even with an individual for engaging in a behavior that we found offensive. However, such anger and grudges eat at individuals' emotional states and cause them to focus on getting even rather than moving on to more productive work.

An all too common practice that happens in school districts is the "blackballing" of some individuals who stand up for their beliefs. Chapter 10 provided a sad example of that happening to a special education teacher. Those who don't agree make a conscious decision to exclude specific individuals from social events, from committees, or from other efforts. Such behavior is not professional. Educators will not always agree with each other but should appreciate the viewpoint of another individual and can "agree to disagree" on an issue without holding a long-term grudge against that person. If you are the victim of blackballing, it is important that you not succumb to pressure or sacrifice your ethics in order to be accepted. You need to hold your head up high and "weather the storm" by remaining true to your beliefs. It may take time, but eventually you as an individual will be respected for your ethical actions.

SUPPORTING YOUR COLLEAGUES WHO EXEMPLIFY THE HIGHEST STANDARDS OF ETHICS

Every day you will have the opportunity to witness individuals who do adhere to the highest standards of ethics—they take strong stands and they do what is right. It is important that we support those individuals in their actions. A supportive e-mail, a friendly visit, talking to them when others won't do so—all of these actions mean a great deal to an individual who is being isolated because he is acting ethically.

THINK AHEAD AND LOOK BACK

In all of our actions, we must look ahead and contemplate the long-term ramifications of our actions. What we do today can impact our own life and the lives of others involved for many years to come. At times we may take an action that is the "path of least resistance." We don't plan on what that will mean in the future to ourselves and to others. As an example, a teacher is stopped by the principal and asked a question about something. The teacher is not sure of the answer but does not want to be perceived as being uninformed. Therefore the teacher gives a definitive answer that impresses the principal immediately. However, the principal learns later that the answer is incorrect and has lost any sense of trust in that teacher. Or in another instance, the principal promises the teacher that she will take action on the teacher's behalf and does not do so. The teacher loses faith in the principal.

In another instance, a teacher serves on a committee to choose a new reading program for the first through third grades. Some of the other members of the committee are impressed with the presentation from one of the publishers, and even though they question the reliability of that reading program, they still want to go with that publisher. Each teacher must look beyond the impressiveness of a presentation and look at the effectiveness of the program. Such a decision is going to impact the lives of children for many years to come.

Individuals tend to be enthralled with some new method or procedure—always looking for the magic bullet that will solve all problems. In an effort to move forward in what they think could be something innovative, they fail to look back at what has been done in the past. Individuals are quick to want to "throw the baby out with the bathwater." The old saying that "history repeats itself" is worth noting. There is a historical perspective about why something is being done the way it is, or there may be a positive lesson that can be learned from history. Educators must both look at what each of their decisions will mean for the future and look back to learn the many lessons that history has to teach us.

REPRESENTING YOURSELF ACCURATELY

As an integral part of our ethical practices, we must continually assess whether we are representing ourselves in an accurate fashion. We must disclose correct information. As part of looking at an issue thoroughly, we must also represent ourselves in a thorough and accurate manner. As was stated earlier, if we are in a position where we have a conflict of interest, we have a moral obligation to disclose that information.

Providing Correct Information about Yourself

Exaggeration can be very easy for someone. We all want to impress others with our knowledge about a subject or about our personal accomplishments. However, we cannot afford to exaggerate our credentials — to do so reduces our credibility, and individuals learn that they are unable to trust us.

We can factually discuss our accomplishments but must do that accurately. An individual reports that he has written 10 articles about a subject. Upon further investigation, it is learned that he has a blog and has made a number of postings on that blog and is counting those as articles. In the publishing world, those would not count as publications. On a resume, we list that we taught at a specific school for four years but fail to mention that we worked there as a substitute, not as a full-time teacher. More on this topic of accurate self-representation is described elsewhere in this book. As part of our call to action, we must monitor that we always accurately present ourselves.

Not Telling the Whole Truth and Nothing but the Truth

One author has encountered multiple situations where individuals in teacher meetings or in educational organizations want to get the group to agree with something that they think should be done. They present information to persuade the group to take their side on the issue. However, they fail to provide all of the information that should be shared with the group for the group members to make an informed decision.

They engage in the process of omission — they don't give information that they believe may result in the group's going against their own opinion. This situation carries a twofold responsibility. The individuals who are making the decision should review written information and ask key questions so they have the entire picture before making a decision. The individual who is trying to persuade the other members of the

group to favor her has a responsibility to provide all the facts and answer questions that are provided. A good clue that someone is not providing all of the information is when the individual becomes defensive
when questions are asked. The ethical individual will provide all the
needed information.

Admitting Possible Conflicts of Interests

As this chapter is being written, a panel of select members of Congress has completed a report that has found that specific educators who
were involved in large federal grants were utilizing the grant money to
promote products for which they received royalties. One individual had
the courage to speak out and state that he must stop what he was doing
because there was a conflict of interest. Other individuals did not show
that courage and were found to have violated conflict-of-interest policies. As a *New York Times* editorial reported:

> Worse still, officials at the Education Department may have known about
> the conflicts and ignored them. As word got around, some state and lo-
> cal officials naturally assumed that the federal government was more in-
> terested in shilling for favored book publishers than in improving read-
> ing instruction for the nation's children. (Editorial, May 19, 2007)

This is a sad case of conflict of interest on a large scale that unfortunately may happen more frequently than we think on a smaller scale
within individual school buildings. This is also indicative of what
sometimes happens—key officials or colleagues know what is going on
and choose to look the other way, thus condoning behavior that is
wrong. When it happens at such a high level, it may snowball and keep
occurring because people begin to think that it is permissible—after all,
the government does it.

Today a colleague of one of the authors shared that he was asked to
be on a panel to read three grant proposals and rank those proposals to
determine which two would be awarded the money. He shared the story
that he immediately disclosed that he knew one of the proposal writers
and therefore must excuse himself from reading the grants because
there would be a conflict of interest.

However, he also voiced his frustration that two other individuals who were asked to read also knew one of the proposal writers and that they had not excused themselves—they failed to reveal a possible conflict of interest. He was in the process of asking the team leader to request that all readers disclose any conflicts of interest they might have by signing a paper stating that they did not know any of the writers. He had been very upset that these two individuals did not disclose this on their own.

It is always important for a person to ask herself whether she may have a conflict of interest that would impact her ability to make a fair and nonbiased decision. Let's look at the example of Natalie. Natalie has been asked to serve on a committee to choose a new assistant principal. However, Natalie's aunt is one of the candidates for the position. Natalie has an obligation to notify the leader of the committee that one of the candidates is her aunt, and she should not be part of the committee to choose the assistant principal.

SUMMARY

Our call to action must involve our commitment to adopt the highest standards of ethics by operating as a fair individual who thinks for himself or herself and makes decisions that are based on sound judgment. Our lives are all about choices, and as Maxwell (2003) states, "Talent is a gift—character is a choice" (p. 44). Professional educators choose to live by a character that is one of the highest standards of ethics.

REFERENCES

Maxwell, J. 2003. *Ethics 101: What every leader needs to know*. New York: Center Street.

Editorial. "Putting more profit before education." *New York Times*, May 19, 2007. www.nytimes.com/2007/05/19/opinion/19sat3.html.

CHAPTER 15

Conclusion: The Ethical Educator—You

The previous chapters opened with a fictitious example used to illustrate the key points of the chapters. *You* are now the story. You must be the one who tells the true story by your own ethical example to others.

You have taken a major step forward in reading this book. Perhaps you read it because you were torn with an ethical dilemma that you have or are currently facing. Join the many educators who daily face those challenges and walk away at the end of the day wondering whether they have done the right thing for children, colleagues, and the profession.

If you are asking yourself questions, you are being proactive and questioning your actions to make sure you are monitoring your own behavior. Our charge is to continually monitor our actions. Keep monitoring your own behavior, establish your standards, and always challenge yourself.

In this summary of the book, we provide you with a set of questions to challenge yourself and your behavior at all times. When faced with an ethical dilemma, challenge yourself to answer these questions. Make questioning a habit for yourself, and you will lead an ethical life in the many facets of your career and personal life.

Can I look the parents of my students in the eye and say this? Put yourself in the parents' place. As a parent, would I want my own child to be treated in this manner? You might also ask whether you could look your own parents in the eye and make the comment. Regardless of our own age and whether our own parents are still living, we are driven by how we have been raised, and most of us want to engage in actions that would meet with our own parents' approval. We do not want to disappoint them and should not want to disappoint a parent of a student by a questionable practice on our part.

Would this stand up in a court of law? In one of the chapters, we discussed that just because something is legal, it doesn't mean that it is ethical. At the same time, the law is a starting point. We must follow the law and the standard established by some courts in determining whether someone is guilty in a dispute: "Am I acting in good faith?" There are times when laws and regulations are not as clear as they should be, and those laws and regulations are up to interpretation. You may have done what you believed the law said, but you should also have been acting in good faith to assure that you believed what you were doing was in the best interest of the student.

Do my words describe my family and coworkers with dignity? We must watch our words very carefully and remember that one word can make a lifelong impact on an individual. In one of the chapters, an author shared the impact that a teacher's calling her work "trite" had on her. Educators must always remember that once they have voiced a word or a sentence, they cannot take it back, and the student, parent, or colleague will remember that word. Therefore, we must think before we speak, and think about the impact of the words we utilize.

Impulsive words uttered or words spoken in anger may be regretted later and more importantly can ruin a relationship that you have worked to build with another individual. However, there will be times when you may voice a thought that you later regret. While you cannot take it back, a strong individual will have the ability to apologize. The power of reflection also allows you to think later about what you have done and how you can change your behavior in the future.

Do I have ways to address my anger and stress so I do not harm my students, family, and coworkers with my behavior? We are all human and face life's many challenges and stresses. We get angry. We become stressed. We may be faced with a deadline or a sick child or parent or both—a child says something to us that we don't want to hear. We snap back at the child, who was very innocent and happened to say the wrong thing at the wrong time. We take our stress or our anger out on the child.

We need to learn stress-reducing activities and anger management—we all know we should take a deep breath and calm down before we say something; this takes continual monitoring on our own part. It also requires us to identify our triggers—what are the behaviors that our students or our colleagues engage in that really "bug us?" All of us have those triggers (some of those are small things, and some are big things)—the student tapping his pencil on the desk, a colleague not doing her part on a project, a student who is late for school every morning.

We have to know what our triggers are and work hard to realize that we are the ones that choose our behavior—if we become upset, we have ourselves to blame. We need to recognize what we can do to not allow others' behaviors to control our own lives.

Does this fit with district policy? Throughout the book, we have talked about the importance of following policies in place in your school district. It is your responsibility to read and know the school district's policy and to follow it. When you have a question about its interpretation, you have an obligation to clarify the meaning with the administrator. Ignorance is no excuse. We all have a responsibility to participate in training about district policy.

We may criticize a policy that contains contents about which we don't agree. Until that policy is changed, we have to follow it. Instead of complaining about the policy, we need to be active members of school or district committees to develop policy.

Would I want my own children to experience this lesson or have this service? One of the authors has experienced the change in a family member's health status. It was not until she had to face medical professionals and advocate for this person that she came to understand more deeply how parents feel. Then, when sitting at the table with families, she realized how important it was to them that she listen carefully and care sincerely about the child's well-being. After all, that is what she wants from the medical professionals who work with her family member.

The family member is the most important person to you at that time. When you are advocating for your own relative, you want your relative to also be the most important person to the people sitting around the table when discussing needs. We should all remember that when we are working with families of the children we serve.

Yes, we are professionals. Yes, we are educators. But we are also sensitive human beings who can pick up on the pain and concern that parents experience. It is essential that we remain open to what matters to them in regard to their children. After all, we would want the same standards in terms of lessons presented and services rendered to our own family.

Is this really true? Being honest is something we instill into students from an early age. We ask them to own up to wrong behavior. We insist that they admit something they did to hurt another student. We require them to tell the truth.

The same holds true for those of us who make such requests of young people. Adults in the school must also be honest. This begins with each individual. Are you honest about your attitudes and feelings relative to your job? Do you speak to students with sincerity relative to their work? Do you tell them when they really need to improve as opposed to sugarcoating your comments? Do you tell parents in a tactful way that the student is having difficulty in certain academic and social areas? Do your comments ring true to your colleagues and administrator? Are you comfortable sharing your struggles as well as your achievements in the school environment?

Honesty is not just about speaking the truth. Honesty is a way of being. It is entering into social and professional exchanges with integrity. Honesty means being able to act according to your instincts and understandings of what is best for each student, parent, colleague, and administrator.

We may think of telling what we consider to be a small lie to save face in a specific situation or to keep from getting in trouble for an action we took. When we do that, we are headed down the wrong path. It becomes very difficult to then remember what you said to which person. Once a colleague or a student catches you not telling the truth, he or she loses any trust in you. Many of us have witnessed an individual who gets into a high-pressure situation and lies about an event.

One of the authors remembers attending a hearing on a legislative issue. The individual who was testifying wanted to "sell" her own position, so she told the committee members a lie—she didn't figure that they would ever know the difference. Maybe they didn't, but the author as an observer knew the information was wrong and never believed the individual again and lost all respect for her.

Do I conduct myself with the same integrity in all professional and personal arenas of my life? In two of the chapters, you learned about two educators who acted very differently when they were at school than they did in their personal lives. They almost had two different personalities. In fact, ethics should characterize our entire lives and should not be something that we turn on and turn off depending on our setting. Educators have a high set of standards that they should meet in all settings. We should be proud to be a part of the teaching profession. When we act with integrity, we can only feel pride in regard to our actions.

Do my values elevate and give dignity to others? Your actions speak louder than words; as you go about your day, let these questions continue to guide you in your actions. You will set a positive example for the students you serve and for all those with whom you come into contact. You will raise the standards for our educational profession and make a positive difference in our world.

We hope you will never have to leave the teaching profession frustrated or self-doubting. If you keep an eye on your own ethical behaviors and you keep refining your ethical knowledge, you will have the utmost satisfaction with your contributions and will retire from the profession with a feeling of success.

Ethical knowledge fades when challenges, dilemmas, and tensions are left unresolved and when you forget how to confront power differentials, fail to address risks of exploitation, can't discern conflicts of interests, don't recognize bias or favoritism, or become self-serving in your actions and encounters.

SUMMARY

This book provides you with a range of concrete examples to explore how ethical issues are conceptualized in education. It also provides you with an examination of how many of these situations are differently and discursively mediated by teachers.

This book also raises the awareness of educators about how ethics are constructed in complex sociopolitical contexts that are sometimes themselves unethical and in conflict and why we, the educators, should become more conscious of the ethical and moral implications of our profession.

We hope that through the sharing of various perspectives, the book has extended the dimensions of your moral understanding of the teaching profession. It is up to you to be the ethical educator.

About the Authors

Beverley H. Johns has more than thirty-five years' experience working with students with significant behavioral disorders and learning disabilities. She is the author or coauthor of nine published books, is active in a number of state and national organizations, and was the 2000 recipient of the Outstanding Leadership Award of the International Council for Exceptional Children.

Mary Z. McGrath taught for thirty-one years, primarily in the area of special education, in Bloomington, Minnesota, public schools. She currently writes and offers varied workshops to educators, parents, and the general public.

Sarup R. Mathur is Clinical Professor, Cluster Chair of the Special Education Program at Arizona State University. She has accumulated extensive experience in developing educational programs for students with special needs. She is interested in the topics of professional development for teachers and high-quality preservice education.